RESPONSIBILITY AND FAULT

RESPONSIBILITY AND FAULT

Tony Honoré

HART PUBLISHING

OXFORD – PORTLAND
2002

HART PUBLISHING
OXFORD AND PORTLAND, OREGON

Published in North America (US and Canada) by
Hart Publishing
c/o International Specialized Book Services
5804 NE Hassalo Street, Portland, Oregon
97213-3644 USA

Hart Publishing is a specialist legal publisher based in Oxford, England. To order further copies of this book or to request a list of other publications please write to:

Hart Publishing, Salter's Boatyard, Folly Bridge,
Abingdon Road, Oxford OX1 4LB
Telephone: +44 (0)1865 245533 or Fax: +44 (0)1865 794882
e-mail: mail@hartpub.co.uk
WEBSITE: http//www.hartpub.co.uk

British Library Cataloguing in Publication
Data Available

ISBN 1 84113-005-2 (cloth)
1 84113-399-X (paper)

Designed by Joe Kenneway, *the big idea*, Oxford
Typeset in 11/13pt Adobe Garamond by Hope Services (Abingdon) Ltd
Printed and bound in Great Britain by Biddles Ltd, Guildford and King's Lynn

To Herbert and John

CONTENTS

1

INTRODUCTION

These essays develop a line of thought that began in the 1950s, when I was working with Herbert Hart on *Causation in the Law* (1st ed. 1959). They are reprinted in chronological order, unaltered apart from the correction of verbal slips. This results in some repetition, but it reveals the development of thought between 1988 and 1998 when the essays were written. The introduction seeks to draw together the various strands.

Hart and I were concerned with the analysis of how ordinary people and lawyers use causal language in assessing liability for conduct and events that cause harm. How does their use of this group of concepts relate to the theories of causation developed by philosophers? Beyond these concerns, I thought at the time, lay a neglected issue. Why should people be held responsible, and so under certain conditions be legally liable, for the harm they cause? That issue involves, and is in the end inseparable from, the question of why people should be held responsible for what they do. It would have taken us too far afield in the 1950s to address this issue. Hart was not at the time keen to pursue it, though in the second edition of our work published in 1985 we did, at my urging, touch on it (pp.lxxx–lxxxi). The essays in this volume explore this and related problems in a way that is, I hope, consistent with the spirit of the original inquiry, though it goes beyond it.

1. Causation

The essays that follow develop the theory that responsibility is something wider than and distinct from moral fault and legal liability, and that being responsible and being legally liable are partly a matter of luck. This theory rests to some extent on the analysis of causation that Hart and I developed. It draws in particular on two aspects of that analysis. One is the idea that to cause something is to intervene in the existing or expected state of the world. The second is the idea that how far back one should go in a causal inquiry depends on the purpose of the inquiry.

After all these years there is still point, it seems, in trying to clarify our theory. For it is not easy to address at the same time the concerns of philosophers and lawyers. Our enterprise was based on the assumption that causation might be an area in which the inquiries of each could illuminate those of the other, despite the fact that some lawyers, in particular judges, have spoken dismissively of the relevance of philosophy to causal issues in the law, and that some philosophers are equally dismissive of the efforts of lawyers. Legal philosophy has to face scepticism on two fronts.

Hart and I believed that, if we drew on the resources of both philosophy and law, it would be possible to show how far in particular cases lawyers' judgements of causal connection rest on specifically legal concerns and how far they draw on a wider concept of causation. This would enable adherents of both disciplines to understand the intricate relation that exists between causal theory and its role in explaining events and assigning responsibility for outcomes.

Our theory of causation drew on several elements in the philosophical tradition. One was the notion, prominent in Hume and Mill, that particular causal statements implicitly appeal to and claim to instantiate empirical generalisations. In our theory this takes the form that a cause is a necessary member of a set of conditions together sufficient to give rise to a given consequence. Essay 5, making use of the analogy of a recipe, seeks to explain why this is to be preferred to the theory that lays the emphasis on a cause as a necessary ("but-for") condition of the consequence in the circumstances.

The strict relation of particular to general holds good, however, only for physical sequences of events. Where, as in law and morals, people are commonly held responsible not merely for initiating physical sequences of events, but for causing, inducing, advising, helping or providing opportunities for others to do harmful (or beneficial) actions, a more relaxed account is needed. The relation between particular and general in these near-causal relationships is partly like but partly unlike that which holds good when purely physical sequences of events are in issue. To act on advice or take advantage of an opportunity instantiates a human trait, and is in that sense an instance of an empirical generalisation. But these relationships can exist in a given instance, even if it is not the case that when similar advice or a similar opportunity is given or presented on another occasion, it will invariably be acted on or exploited by the person to whom it was given previously or by others. I may succeed today in persuading you to invest in Eldorado Mines, though my advice would not persuade others to do so and would not convince you next week. The same applies to the negative relationships, important in law and morals, of not providing information or opportunities on which another person could act to their benefit. For example, a doctor may fail to disclose the risk associated with proposed surgical treatment to a patient who would have been deterred by knowledge of the risk. A seller may fail to deliver goods on time to a buyer who would have made a profit had they been available.

These near-causal relationships are related to one another and to the causal paradigm of initiating physical sequences of events, in that they resemble them in some respects and can in some conditions found moral blame and legal liability. This illustrated, we thought, points made by the later Wittgenstein in his treatment of family resemblance. Like members of a family, the various types of near-causal relationship differ among themselves. For example, does the agent whose liability is in question provide another with a reason or an opportunity to act or does the agent help another to act? If the agent provides a reason, is it one that most people would regard as compelling, in which case the agent would naturally be said to have *caused* the other to act as he does? Or is it one that the other regards as sufficient to persuade him to act on this occasion, though another person, or the same person on another occasion, might not do so? These relationships also differ in their degree of deviation from the central case of initiating a physical sequence of events. The generalisations to which they implicitly appeal may be more or less rigorous and the incidence of liability wider or narrower.

We also drew on the pragmatic tradition associated with writers such as Collingwood in England and F.S. Cohen in the United States. They pointed out that what counts as the cause of an event depends on the purpose of the inquiry. Someone is killed in a road accident. Was the cause of his death internal bleeding, the driver's mistake, the ice on the road with which the driver failed to cope, or the shortage of funds that led to the local authority's not removing the ice in time?

All these could be necessary members of a set of conditions sufficient to bring about the victim's death; so they could all count as causes of that death. Which is picked out as the cause in a given context depends on how far back the inquiry is taken,[1] and this in turn depends on its purpose. Is it medical or legal? Is it concerned with road safety or local authority funding? In a legal context the aim of a causal inquiry is usually narrow.[2] It is focussed on discovering whether a particular action, generally of an unlawful character,[3] caused a particular item of harm of a type recognised by law. A legal inquiry is not an inquiry at large into the cause or causes of an untoward or unexplained event.

Moreover, the context of legal liability restricts the way in which the causal issue is formulated. In law a plaintiff or prosecutor must normally allege that the fact that a defendant did an action of such-and-such a type caused a consequence of such-and-such a type to occur. *What* has to be alleged and proved is a matter of law, since law settles the types of conduct and outcome for which a legal remedy is available. Law also settles whether the basis of liability is to be fault, strict liability or insurance or whether, though one person has harmed another, the agent incurs no legal liability. Take, for instance, liability in tort law for fault. If the action is for damages for physical injury caused by negligence, the plaintiff must show, for example, that the fact that the defendant failed to keep a proper lookout was the cause of the fact that the plaintiff suffered a leg injury. The events between which causal connection must be proved must be described in such a way as to fall within the appropriate legal category. Failing to keep a proper lookout is an instance of negligent conduct by the driver of a car, and a leg injury is an instance of physical injury.

In a legal context, then, law determines *what* has to be proved to have caused *what*.[4] But to judge *whether* one thing has caused another is, lawyers in the common law tradition assert, largely a matter of

1. It also depends on the principle adopted for selecting causes from a complex of conditions, as to which see p.6 below.
2. Not always. There are sometimes judicial inquiries into the causes of air and rail disasters and other untoward happenings.
3. In the case of strict liability the action is not unlawful and in cases of insurance law the inquiry may be whether certain stereotyped conditions, such as marine risks, caused damage.
4. There is now a good judicial exposition of this point by Lord Hoffmann in *Environment Agency* v. *Empress Car Co (Abertillery) Ltd* [1998] 2 WLR 350, 358.

applying to the facts the ordinary person's understanding of the concept of cause. This analysis seemed to Hart and me broadly correct in the fifties and still seems so today. It is true that ordinary people are not familiar with the idea of a necessary member of a set of conditions together sufficient to bring about a given outcome. Nor could they give a theoretical account of what it is to intervene in the existing or expected state of affairs. But, because causal judgements are so pervasive a feature of everyday life, ordinary people learn to apply the concept of cause with reasonable accuracy, just as most of us can drive a car or operate a computer without being able to give a convincing account of the way they work. Hence, we argued, many decisions in different jurisdictions and different branches of the law (torts, contracts, criminal law) reflect the theory outlined. In this connection we appealed to the methods of linguistic philosophy that were fashionable in the fifties and sixties. Much can be learned, it was thought, about the nature of a concept and its variants by studying the way in which it is used by ordinary people who are familiar with it. Their use of language when describing events will mark empirical differences, even subtle differences, in the world they describe. Moreover, a distinction that is deeply embedded in our thought and language, like the distinction between acts and omissions (essay 3), probably serves a worthwhile function if we can but discover what it is. The fact that law is addressed to, and meant to be understood by, ordinary people is an added reason why lawyers should treat causal issues as issues of fact and should pay attention to the difference between cases where it is natural to say that one person caused another to act in a harmful way, and those where it is more natural to speak of persuading, recommending, making possible, or helping another so to act. These verbal distinctions offer a clue to significant differences of fact.

The changes that have occurred in philosophy since the fifties do not seem to invalidate this method of analysis, though it certainly needs to be supplemented. In particular, attention must be directed to the justification in normative contexts for making use of the distinctions we find reflected in ordinary language. And it must be conceded that, at the margin, common sense judgements of causal or near-causal connection are in legal practice sometimes modified or overridden by the purpose of the legal provision on which the claim is based and by the wish to do justice in the particular circumstances. The harm for which a remedy is given must not only be caused by the defendant's action but must fall within the purpose of the rule of law violated and the plaintiff must not be morally disentitled to pursue the remedy. Given that all laws have limited aims, even if these are not always easy to ascertain, and that they typically claim to impose morally binding obligations, it could not be otherwise.

Finally, there was an element of our work that did not rest, so far as I can judge, on any previous or contemporary philosophical tradition. This concerned the selection of the cause from the set of conditions together sufficient to bring about the consequence. We argued that those conditions that are abnormal in the context, along with voluntary (in the sense of free and deliberate) human actions, have a prior claim to be selected as causes of an unexplained event. These conditions have on the whole greater explanatory power than others. What the two (the abnormal and the voluntary) have in common is that they are, or can be regarded as, interventions in the world. They bring about changes in the existing or expected state of affairs. This feature confers on them explanatory force. But whereas, for example, scientific explanation usually proceeds from outcome to cause, law moves in the opposite direction, from cause to outcome. For it is in general concerned with determining the extent of liability for an unlawful action that is taken as proved rather than with explanation as such. Hence, in legal contexts, the priority of abnormal events and of free and deliberate human actions as causes is typically shown in a different way. Priority is given to these factors not in explaining how harm has come about but in fixing the limits of liability for actions that the law has designated as potential sources of liability. Later interventions, whether free and deliberate actions or abnormal events, are very often regarded as cutting short liability and so limiting what the original agent is taken to have done. In relation to both explanation and the assessment of liability, then, the concept of a cause as an intervention that changes the existing or expected state of affairs, and human action as something that starts and ends with such an intervention, is fundamental. There are, indeed, near-causal types of liability, such as liability for providing opportunities to do good or harm, that override these limits. But they are, both morally and legally, marginal in relation to the overall picture.

It seems, then, at most a half truth that law is not concerned with philosophical theories of causation. What tempts some lawyers to assert the contrary is that law is more often engaged in fixing the limits of liability than with explanation as such, whereas science concentrates on explanation and history is concerned with both. Moreover, law sets the limits within which causation is an element in legal disputes. Within those limits legal systems take account, in determining the extent of liability, not merely of causal or near-causal connection, but of the elements of justice (corrective, distributive and retributive), that fall to be considered when legal liability in its various forms is assessed. People are never legally liable *merely* because they have caused someone harm.

2. Responsibility

Justice in these different forms, however, presupposes that people are responsible for what they do and, within the limits set by later intervention, for the outcome of what they do. That is not a self-evident truth. We do not have complete control over our actions. Sometimes we do things that we do not mean to. Often what we do has consequences that we did not intend or foresee. Any good argument for making people responsible for what they do or cause (outcome responsibility, as I have termed it) must show why to hold them responsible is not only just but is in their interest and in the general interest.

A start on this theme was made in essay 2, on Responsibility and Luck (1988). I there argued that people are responsible for their actions and the unintended outcome of their actions even when not morally to blame.

This and the later essays cite legal examples. The reason for this is not just the wish to make the argument more persuasive to lawyers, though it is important for legal philosophers to attend to the conceptual worries of lawyers. A good reason for citing legal examples in support of the argument is that, on one view of the relations between law and morals, legal examples are often likely to be carefully thought out in their moral implications and hence to be morally persuasive.

My view of the relations, or some relations, between law and morals, can only be touched on here. It differs from Hart's. Hart argued for a more rigorous separation of law and morals than seems plausible even in a purely descriptive enterprise. I think that when laws confer rights or impose obligations they *purport* to confer morally reputable entitlements and to impose morally binding obligations. As a result, one type of argument that is in point when lawyers interpret authoritative sources (such as statutes, judicial decisions, and treaties) is that, if taken at face value, they would lead to morally objectionable results. For this reason arguments of equity, justice and other moral values are an organic, not merely an incidental, feature of legal systems. In practice, these arguments do not uniformly prevail in legal proceedings, nor should they. But it is always open to those who have to argue or decide what the law is to have recourse to them. Moreover, many legal rules (not only those that purport to solve problems of co-ordination) are morally binding only because imposed by law.[5] There is an important area in which laws seek to give effect in detail to general moral principles, but the influence is not all in one direction. The effect of legal determinations of moral principle is often to make them obligatory *as part of morality*, quite apart from any general presumption there may be in favour of a moral duty to obey the law. This is because some moral obligations can only exist when more precisely defined than is possible by deduction from moral principles alone. Moreover, some principles, such as the principle that the person who stands to profit from a certain transaction must bear the risk of any loss that may arise from it, have been developed and refined in legal contexts, yet possess independent moral force. These connections between law and morality, if they exist, do not force one to take sides in the largely sterile controversy between positivism and natural law. But they show that legal examples can have moral weight, and can with due caution be cited in philosophical argument.

To return to the theme of Responsibility and Luck, that essay starts from the rule that many systems of law impose civil (and sometimes criminal) liability for failure to observe an objective standard of care, for example in driving a car. The argument is that this rule, though said to be based on fault, imposes liability on people for conduct that at times cannot plausibly be said to be their fault. The law makes them pay for actions attributable to defects such as stupidity and clumsiness of which they cannot rid themselves, certainly not in the short run. Their situation is then not morally different from that of

5. T. Honoré, "The Dependence of Morality on Law", 13 *Oxford Journal of Legal Studies* (1993) 1–17.

people held strictly liable in tort (and to a lesser extent in criminal law) when they undertake some permitted but dangerous activity, like using explosives, that results in damage despite the care they take to avoid it. Are those held liable in this way being treated solely as a means to the social goal of reducing accidents, in the way that Kant condemns? Or can strict liability sometimes be morally justified?

I contend that it can be, since we are responsible for what we do, including what we do without intending to, or without foreseeing the consequences.[6] And if we are responsible for what we do and its outcome, even in the absence of fault, the state, as representing the community, is sometimes justified in attaching to actions that are not morally blameworthy a duty to pay compensation or a fine. While it is permissible to pursue the dangerous activity, it is not in order to refuse to pay for the consequences. Strict liability in law, when imposed in a collective interest such as that of reducing accidents, builds on people's basic responsibility for their actions. Our responsibility for actions and outcomes requires us to bear the risk of bad luck both in the way we are constituted and in the external circumstances in which we find ourselves. This may extend to the risk of having to pay for harm that we inflict without fault. At the same time the system of responsibility enables us to profit from good luck if what we do turns out better than we intended or foresaw. Human action invites assessment, and the credit we receive from what turns out well balances the discredit we incur for what turns out badly. We cannot take the credit without the discredit, since that would be to violate the principle of taking the rough with the smooth – a principle that possesses moral force and can perhaps be regarded as a form of distributive justice (risk-distributive justice).

The system of responsibility is in most people's interest. If they possess normal capacities, they succeed and take credit for their success more than they fail and incur discredit for their failures. They bet, as it were, on the outcome of their actions, and win more than they lose. But for the "incapable", who are immature, mentally deranged, or abnormally incompetent the balance may be unfavourable. Morality and law take account of this, but not by denying that the incapable are responsible for actions that are genuinely theirs and go to form

6. This is the basic form of responsibility. The responsibility that we take on for other people and things, or that is thrust on us by society, is analysed in essay 6.

their character. Instead morality and law limit the consequences of their responsibility. They treat the incapable as free (or relatively free) from moral blame and exempt (or partially exempt) from legal liability. "Diminished responsibility" refers to the situation of people who are responsible for their actions but are not exposed to all the normal consequences, legal and moral, of that responsibility.

We should be slow to deny responsibility to those who suffer from incapacity. Though it may be fair, for reasons to be discussed, to attach less blame to those who have less capacity to control their actions, and to mitigate their legal liability, to deny people's responsibility for their actions is to strike at their identity. The best argument for outcome responsibility is surely that it is central to the identity and character of the agent. This point is developed particularly in essays 4 and 5, where I contend that our responsibility for what we do and for its outcome is inseparable from our status as persons. We are the people we are and have the character we have largely because the dealings in which our bodies and brains are involved, if in some aspect intentional, are attributed to us as the actions of persons with a continuing identity. This attribution depends on the view of causation according to which our interventions in the world are cut short by later interventions, so that each person has a set of achievements or failures that is exclusively their own or is shared with a few others.

We might, as a logical possibility, abandon this way of thinking and treat what people appear to do as *exclusively* determined by their background, heredity, environment, temperament and other circumstances. Their "actions" would be stages in a mechanism set in motion by earlier events – though, as an *exclusive* point of view, I think this would be psychologically impossible. We cannot, however, be sure that some form of determinism is not true. At times we think of our own and other people's conduct as determined or strongly influenced by external and internal factors. Yet a general adoption of this as the exclusive way of thinking about human conduct, even if possible, would be against our interest. People's interests lie in accepting responsibility for what they do even when they make mistakes or do the wrong thing or fail to foresee the consequences of their conduct. Accepting responsibility for our actions makes for a better society because it encourages us to do well and to enjoy the credit that comes from doing well. Above all, the system of responsibility is essential to our self-respect and our respect for others.

Nor, if determinism in some form turns out to be true, have we made a mistake in treating ourselves as responsible for our actions. How far one should go back in a causal inquiry depends on the purpose of the inquiry. To treat people as the authors of and responsible for their actions is necessary if we value a society of individuals who respect themselves and one another. To uphold that value it is rational, as a general policy, to treat people as responsible even if their capacity to control their conduct is restricted or they are subject to strong pressures to reject social norms.

This does not imply that an agent's capacity to control his conduct is irrelevant to his moral culpability or legal liability. On the contrary, as is argued in essay 5 and recognised in many areas of criminal law, the handicaps to which offenders are subject are relevant to the extent to which they deserve to be punished. To that extent law and morality give effect to the retributive principle that the penalty should not be disproportionate to the moral gravity of the offence. The agent's degree of control over his conduct affects his freedom, positive and negative. His degree of freedom is relevant to the gravity of the offence he commits. Even if determinism is in some form true, the degree to which people are capable of conforming to law varies.

But determinism does raise a familiar spectre. I have assumed that moral blame and legal liability depend partly on the agent's capacity for self-control and the extent to which the agent is free. But if no one can do anything other than what they do, is not everyone's (in)capacity the same? So can anyone be responsible or to blame? Responsibility has been discussed. The arguments for it remain unaffected by the non-existent capacity of the agent, if that is what determinism entails. For the system of responsibility will still encourage self-respect and act as an incentive to do well. The second point, however, about fault, raises an important issue about the link between capacity and blame. Capacity is assumed to be relevant to blame and to legal liability. If everyone has the same (in)capacity, then should not everyone be open to blame and to legal liability to the same extent as everyone else? This conclusion depends, in my view, on a misunderstanding of what we understand by capacity. In essay 6 an article of 1964 is reprinted in which, in the idiom of the time, the argument is made that, in morals and law, capacity means a person's *general* capacity to perform successfully the type of action that he failed to perform on this occasion. It does not refer to a capacity in the specific circumstances to do something other than what the agent did (*particular* capacity). Moral blame and legal liability depend on general, not particular capacity. This view has the consequence that, when we act, we take the risk of not performing up to our normal capacity on a given occasion. Since people do not have complete control over what they do, human action always involves risk-taking, and one of the risks we take when we act is that of incurring blame or liability because we fall short of our normal level of achievement. Determinism, if true, cannot alter the fact that people's general capacities vary and with it their freedom of action, including the range of choices open to them. It is not easy to say *why* moral blame should be affected by the agent's relative capacity and freedom. Perhaps the reason is that the system of responsibility has a competitive aspect, and those who suffer from incapacity are handicapped as competitors in life's struggle.

The discussion has so far been concerned with positive acts (actions). But what has been said extends also by analogy to responsibility for omissions. Essay 3 is concerned with this theme. A non-action or failure to act can be treated as an intervention in the world, and so as a cause whenever a positive act is expected or required but the agent does not perform it. The change thus brought about is a change not in the existing but in the expected state of affairs. If there is a norm requiring positive action the non-performance of the act is treated as an omission and brings in its train responsibility. This may lead to moral blame or legal liability if the non-performance is open to moral criticism or is contrary to law. The essay examines the common view, challenged by some philosophers, that positive acts are worse than omissions even when the two bring about equally serious harm. It concludes that this view is false when the agent (or failed agent) has a special duty towards the person harmed, but is true when he does not. When the agent has no special duty to the person harmed, the difference between positive acts and omissions is connected with the difference between making another person's position worse and not making it better.

Two of the essays are concerned to apply the theory of outcome responsibility to tort law and criminal law. Essay 4 disentangles various questions about the justification for imposing liability in tort law. It makes the point that, whereas tort law ultimately forces us to pay compensation for the harmful outcome of conduct for which we are responsible, the class of cases in which it is entitled to do this depends on considerations of corrective, distributive and retributive justice. Outcome responsibility is a condition of corrective justice, but the justification of outcome responsibility depends in part on the justice of allocating responsibility according to risk, which is a matter of distributive justice. The principle of retribution sets limits to the extent to which it is proper for the law to sanction corrective justice by imposing a duty to compensate in tort law, but, given that the sanctions of tort law are pecuniary, these limits are less stringent than in criminal law.

Essay 6 addresses a paradox in the criminal process. People are, with few exceptions, regarded as responsible for the offences they commit, at least when the issue is guilt or innocence. But when the law is concerned with the seriousness of the offence (e.g. murder or manslaughter) or the appropriate punishment, the fact that the offender was not fully capable of behaving rationally, because subject to various forms of stress such as provocation, addiction, emotional disturbance or the like, is treated as relevant. I defend this broad distinction on the ground that it is important both to the offender and others not to deny the offender's responsibility for what has been done. On the other hand, punishment should take account of the retributive principle according to which the sanction should not be disproportionate to blame. Those who are less able to control their conduct suffer a handicap in relation to those who are better able to do so, and are correspondingly less to blame for their failures than the better placed. According to this line of thought, the criminal process should openly recognise that offenders who come from a socially or morally deprived background have fewer options open to them, and less capacity for self-control than others more fortunately situated. Their relative lack of freedom is something properly taken into account in sentencing.

The dedication is to two legal philosophers, one older and one younger, with whom I have had the pleasure of collaborating over many years.

2

RESPONSIBILITY AND LUCK
THE MORAL BASIS OF STRICT LIABILITY

This essay[1] touches on both civil and common law, but its central theme is a very broad one: that being responsible in law and in ordinary life is not the same thing as being at fault or to blame. It starts from the well-known rule of the tort of negligence that requires everyone to attain an objective standard of care and competence; and then moves towards a theory of responsibility in which the contrast between fault and strict liability, though not obliterated, is blunted.

The argument is in three sections. As it is a little complicated, I summarise it at the start. The first section argues that the objective standard of competence, though purporting to be based wholly on fault, really imposes a form of strict liability on those who suffer from unavoidable shortcomings. In the absence of a moral justification for strict liability it cannot be supported.

To justify strict liability we must first show why people should sometimes bear the risk of bad luck, including in bad luck such misfortunes as being stupid or clumsy. The second section argues that to bear the risk of bad luck is inherent in the basic form of responsibility in any society, which I term outcome responsibility. Outcome responsibility means being responsible for the good and harm we bring about by what we do. By allocating credit for the good outcomes of actions and discredit for bad ones, society imposes outcome responsibility; though often the rewards it attaches and, outside the law, the sanctions it imposes are informal and vague. Under a system of outcome responsibility we are forced, if we want to keep our social account in balance, to make what amounts to a series of bets on our choices and their outcomes. Provided we have a minimum capacity

1. A version of the 13th Blackstone lecture delivered in Oxford under the auspices of Pembroke College on 8 May 1988. First published in 104 *Law Quarterly Review* (1988) pp.530–53.

for choosing and acting, we win the bets and get credit for good outcomes more than we lose them and incur discredit for bad ones. We have to take the risk of harmful outcomes that may be sheer bad luck and not our fault; but that does not make the system unfair to people who are likely to be winners overall.

Seen in this light civil liability in law, whether strict or based on fault, can be defended on the ground that it specifies an extra sanction to be imposed on a person who has anyhow lost a bet and will in consequence incur discredit. The main role of legal liability is to reinforce our basic outcome responsibility with formal sanctions such as compensation or punishment. One ground for legal liability, fault, is present when the person's conduct not only has a bad outcome but displays a bad disposition. Another, which leads to strict liability, is present when the activity that has a bad outcome is specially dangerous to others. In practice these grounds often overlap.

Can the system of outcome responsibility itself be justified or shown to be inescapable? Outcome responsibility is, I contend, inescapable because it is the counterpart and at the same time a constituent of our personal identity and character. We could not dispense with outcome responsibility without ceasing to be persons.

The third section deals with capacity and freedom. Outcome responsibility, though inescapable, can fairly be imposed only on those who possess a sufficient general capacity for decision and action. Capacity can for this purpose be tested by asking what a given person normally achieves when he tries. It has, however, often been thought that responsibility for a particular action requires something further; a capacity on the part of the person to have acted differently given all the factors, external and internal, that were present on the occasion in question. But this sort of anti-deterministic capacity cannot exist. So my theory of responsibility, though it does not require determinism to be true, is compatible with it. The difference between fault and strict liability in this respect is merely that a person guilty of fault must have, besides a general capacity for decision and action, the ability to succeed most of the time in doing the sort of thing that would on this occasion have averted the harm. A person held strictly liable must have the same general capacity but need not have this special ability.

1. Negligence: The Objective Standard of Competence

The starting point of the argument is one that at first sight has nothing to do with strict liability. It is the familiar rule of the law of negligence that everyone is bound to reach an objective standard of care and competence. One corollary is that a person is liable for substandard conduct, or is prejudiced by it, even if he acts as he does because of a shortcoming that he cannot help. A stupid lorry-driver fails to slow down in the fog and has an accident. One of normal intelligence would have slowed down and avoided it. An impetuous pedestrian dashes across the street and is run over. A more equable person would have waited and walked across safely. An inexperienced surgeon cuts an artery that with greater experience he would have known how to avoid. In view of the objective theory of negligence, their respective shortcomings (stupidity, impetuousness, perhaps also inexperience) make them legally liable or reduce their claims.[2]

Some explanation of the terms employed may be useful. "Negligence" refers to civil liability, in whatever system, for unintended harm, where this is caused by someone's failure to meet the required standard of competence. The liability may be in tort or delict, for breach of contract, under a special statute or under more than one of these at once. Negligence, the common law term, is here used in a transsystematic way, as equivalent to Roman *culpa*, German *Fahrlässigkeit*, and French *faute de négligence*. Lack of competence may stem from a number of factors. The person concerned, for whom the term "shortcomer" is to hand, may not have the qualities, physical, intellectual or emotional, needed to attain the standard set for the task in question. He may lack the proper makeup. He may suffer from a defect of character, temperament or physique, limited intelligence, accident proneness, bad co-ordination, slow reactions. On the other hand he may possess the physical and mental equipment but lack education or training. Or he may have had all these but, as a child, lack maturity, or, as a novice, experience. The shortcomer's lack of competence may thus stem from a defect of physique

2. For inexperience the issue is debated: *Nettleship* v. *Weston* [1971] 2 QB 691; *Wilsher* v. *Essex Health Authority* [1987] QB 730.

or character, or a deficiency in intelligence, learning or experience. Shortcoming comprises these defects and deficiencies.

The objective theory of negligence, which is orthodox in the leading systems of law,[3] requires people to display the same competence as a hypothetical model person. To bring in a model person is to translate a normative standard into a hypothetical descriptive standard. The model is variously depicted in different legal cultures. He or she is seen as a diligent father, a reasonable man/woman, an abstract type,[4] or a careful and conscientious member of the class in question.[5] The class may, according to the case, be that of doctor, driver, company director, air pilot,[6] pedestrian etc. The classification depends on the type of person expected to undertake the task performance of which goes wrong (operating, driving, running a business, crossing the street), and to display care or skill in doing so.[7] The objective standard has, on the orthodox view, to be met both in avoiding harm to others and in protecting oneself.[8] Failure to meet it may either make the injurer liable to pay damages as defendant or may bar the injured, in whole or in part, from recovering damages as plaintiff.

Such is the general law. It applies, however, only to persons who have capacity, a notion distinct from competence. The incapable are not held to it. In most systems a child is regarded as wholly or partly

3. E.g. F.V. Harper, F.I. James and O.S. Gray, *The Law of Torts* (2nd ed. 1986) vol. III p.103f.; A. Weill and F. Terré, *Droit Civil des Obligations* (4th ed. 1986) s.628; E. Deutsch, *Haftungsrecht: Allgemeine Lehre* (1976) p.268f. In Germany the objective theory is statutory. BGB s.276 lays down that a person subject to a duty acts negligently is he fails to take account of the care required by (social) intercourse: *die im Verkehr erforderliche Sorgfalt ausser acht lässt.*
4. As French lawyers put it.
5. The German formulation.
6. Viz. an ordinary air pilot, not a pilot "having the same training and experience as Fred Heath": *Heath* v. *Swift Wings Inc.* 40 NC App. 158, 252 SE 2d 526, 529 (1979).
7. This is the answer to Nipperdey's objection that the class selected might equally be that of the phlegmatic, cholerics, alcoholics, etc. Staudinger, *BGB* s.276 no.18. The class test is not alien to English law: *The Lady Gwendolen* [1965] P. 294 (reasonable shipowner); *Philips* v. *Whiteley* [1938] 1 All ER 566 (reasonable jeweller); *Wilsher* v. *Essex Health Authority* [1987] QB 730 (duty of doctor relates to post which he occupies, not his own qualifications and experience).
8. Some have argued that the incapable should, in protecting themselves, be judged by a more subjective standard (Harper, James and Gray, above n.3, vol. III pp.462–4); H.H. Terry, 29 *Harvard Law Rev.* (1914–5) 47; *Dellwo* v. *Pearson* 259 Minn. 452, 107 NW 2d 859, 862–3 (1961), rejected in *Dunn* v. *Teti* 280 Pa. Super 399, 421 Atl. 2d 782, 784 (1980).

incapable, in some the insane,[9] in some the elderly.[10] The incapable may be exempt altogether, or required to meet a standard adjusted to their limitations. Then there are special cases where even a person of full capacity has only to do as much as he can,[11] or as much as he does when occupied with his own affairs.[12] The objective standard gives way to a subjective or mixed standard.

This outline of the law provides the background to what follows. Historically negligence, like intentional wrongdoing, has been regarded as a species of fault. Nearly all writers continue so to regard it, and the equivalent terms in other systems (*culpa*, *Fahrlässigkeit*, etc.) all connote fault. According to a long-standing opinion, which provisionally I adopt, fault is imputed only to a person who could have controlled the situation in which he was placed but failed to do so. Only someone who *could in the circumstances have acted otherwise* is morally responsible, and, if necessary, blamed for his action.[13] This view is open to challenge; and on a narrow interpretation of "could" or a wide interpretation of "circumstance" I shall argue that it should be rejected.[14] But there is no doubt that the "could have done otherwise" test appeals powerfully to both lawyers and philosophers. Apply that test to the law of negligence, and a person is at fault only when he could observe the objective standard, but fails to do so. So the incompetent shortcomer who fails to come up to standard is not at fault and should not be held guilty of negligence. There is linguistically an exception when the incompetence is due to a defect, or as it is often called, "fault" of character. But though on a long term view it

9. Some cases allow mental subnormality to reduce the standard expected: e.g. *Miller* v. *Trinity Medical Center* 260 NW 2d 4, 6–7 (1977).

10. Elderly plaintiff: e.g. *Johnson* v. *St Paul City R Co* 67 Minn. 260, 69 NW 900,901 (1897).

11. E.g. because he is confronted with a situation that is not of his choosing, like a fire which through no fault of his breaks out on his land: *Goldman* v. *Hargrave* [1967] 1 AC 645. This duty to do what you can (*eigenmögliche Sorgfalt*: Deutsch, above n.3, at p.280), which in German law applies to matters such as the award of a solatium for death, injury or loss of liberty (*BGB* s.847 Schmerzengeld) is to be distinguished from the degree of care which the agent, who may have fallen into a slack routine, normally gives to his own affairs (below n.12).

12. The civil law *diligentia quam in suis rebus*, which applied to transactions like gratuitous deposit, where it seemed unreasonable to demand that the depositee should take greater care of his friend's property than his own. *BGB* s.277 and commentaries provide modern examples.

13. E.g. A.J. Ayer, *Philosophical Essays* (1954) p.27.

14. Below pp.32–8.

may be possible to correct some faults of character, or to avoid acquiring them in the first place, in any immediate or short-term context a faulty character is something with which the person concerned has to cope much as he has to cope with a faulty engine. Moreover, the law treats as fault other sorts of incompetence due to, say, stupidity or clumsiness, which the person clearly cannot correct in time, and perhaps not ever.[15]

Can this be justified? On one line of argument the shortcomer is not morally to blame but reasons of policy justify us in treating him as responsible. A consequentialist may argue that it is right to impose objective liability because to do so maximises either average or minimum utility, wealth, satisfaction of preferences or some other good. The rule of objective liability tends to increase economic efficiency, or to redistribute resources in favour of accident victims in a desirable way. But though these may be reasons for sustaining the rule, if it can independently be shown to be fair, what justification is there for pursuing these aims by imposing liability on those who are not at fault? After all, in criminal law we think it is only those who have consciously made a wrong choice whom we can properly treat, within limits, as fair game: as instruments of general deterrence, who need not be regarded solely as ends in themselves but in part as means to enhance the security of others.[16] Why should it be different in civil law? It is true that the sanction in civil law is to pay money, not go to prison. The stigma is less. But we do not think that in criminal law the innocent who lack *mens rea* should be fined rather than imprisoned. We think they should be acquitted.

Another pragmatic argument for the objective standard concerns proof. It is hard to prove that the person concerned has not done as much to avoid harming himself or others as he could have done. Failure to meet the objective standard is easier to prove, since we have by experience an intuitive idea of how to apply that standard. We reckon to know how a reasonable motorist drives a car but, unless we

15. Harper, James and Gray, above n.3, vol. III p.104; H. and L. Mazeaud and A. Tunc, *Responsabilité Civile* (6th ed. 1965) vol. I ss.418f, distinguish social and moral from legal fault, the latter including cases that I would regard as coming within strict liability, since the mark of fault is that it reflects adversely on the character or disposition of the agent.

16. There are of course those who deny that to treat the guilty as means in this way is morally permissible, or who advance (unconvincing) arguments to the effect that punishment does not involve this.

know his driving very well, find it almost impossible to fix the standard of which a particular motorist is capable.

It is true that the objective standard makes proof easier and so saves trouble and cost. In applying any normative standard it is convenient to be guided by conventional practices, though these are clearly not immune from criticism. Practice may be slack, as in the case of those pilots who allegedly navigate car ferries without verifying that the doors are closed. But often practice serves to settle, at least provisionally, the content of the objective standard.[17]

The difficulty of proof has some weight in support of the objective standard, but by itself hardly provides a compelling reason for it. Moreover, in criminal law the difficulty of proving intention, often considerable, does not let in proof of a standard or model intention instead of the actual intention of the defendant.

Another argument for objective liability is that any unfairness there may be in holding the shortcomer to an objective standard is minor in extent. Civil liability is often covered by third-party insurance, for example, motor insurance. A person who is insured suffers less than if he had to pay from his own pocket. So, it is said, in these cases the objective standard does not impose much hardship. But the objective standard existed in the ancient world and continued in force for many centuries before third-party insurance became a widespread, though certainly not universal, practice. Has the justification for it sprung into being in the industrial age? Moreover, the insurance argument, which applies only to those walks of life in which insurance is the standard or required practice, merely displaces the question. Why should a person who commits no fault be burdened with insurance premiums?

The various consequentialist arguments of social and legal policy so far adduced seem not to provide an adequate reason for imposing objective liability in the absence of a moral justification of a non-consequentialist sort. The arguments they provide are supplementary rather than basic. What is in issue is the justice of objective liability, not merely its expediency. Is it fair to the individuals concerned to hold them responsible for their shortcomings? The good consequences may be necessary, but hardly sufficient reasons for doing so.

---

17. For a similar point in regard to the standard for children, see the good discussion in *Tyler* v. *Weed* 285 Mich. 460, 280 NW 827 (1938).

What justifications of this more ambitious sort are on offer? Perhaps the Roman jurist Gaius was the first to rationalise the objective theory of unintentional fault, a theory which is an invention of law, not philosophy.[18] He starts from the Case of the Weak Muleteer:

> "A muleteer who lacks the skill to restrain his mules, so that they crush a slave, is ordinarily said to be liable for fault. The same applies if he is too weak to restrain them. Nor does it appear unjust to count infirmity as fault, since no one should undertake a task when he knows or should know that his infirmity will make its execution dangerous to others".[19]

To rebut the argument that the muleteer whose lack of skill or strength causes harm is not at fault, since, given his infirmity, he could not avoid the harm, Gaius argues that the muleteer was at fault at an earlier stage.[20] It was this prior fault, he implies, which consisted in undertaking a task for which he was not equipped, that made the later accident inevitable. It was a fault because the muleteer knew or should have known of his own incompetence before he took the mules on the road.

Is this argument persuasive? If the muleteer knew he was incompetent fault was indeed, by our ordinary criteria of judgement, present. He knowingly courted danger for himself and others. But if he did not appreciate his own incompetence, what is the force of the assertion that he "should have known" of it? Perhaps he was too obtuse to realise his own infirmity, and no one pointed it out. In his own eyes he was an ace muleteer. If he then has to pay for the accident he is paying for his defective makeup, not for fault.

Like Gaius, we can generalise the muleteer case. It is not true that a person who undertakes a task for which he is not up to scratch need be at fault in failing to realise the fact. Lack of skill often goes hand in hand with lack of the nous to recognise one's incompetence. Prior fault can serve to justify only some of the cases in which legal systems impose liability for lack of competence. Can some other theory justify the rest?

---

18. D. Daube, *Roman Law: Linguistic, Social and Philosophical Aspects* (1969) pp.131, 151f. It is true that Aristotle set up the model of a zealous person (*spoudaios*), and provided a theory of how people are ultimately responsible for their characters. But to expound and seek to justify the objective standard is to take a further step.
19. *Digest* 9.2.8.1 (Gaius 7 ed. prov.). Essentially the same argument appears in *Wilsher* v. *Essex Health Authority* [1987] QB 730, 777C per Browne-Wilkinson VC.
20. A species of introductory or disabling fault (*einleitender Fahrlässigkeit*): Deutsch, above n.3, at p.280.

One possibility is promising. At times the person whose conduct is sub-standard has made an express or implied promise to reach the model standard. The surgeon may put himself forward as expert in heart by-passes, the lorry driver as capable of driving a snow-plough in bad weather. It may then be legitimate to infer that they are promising to perform up to their assumed expertise when they operate on X or clear Y's land. But they need not and usually do not promise to reach the objective standard. Thus, most newly qualified doctors do not pretend to years of practice. On the whole professional people allow others to assume in them certain skills, but make no specific claim, and fight shy of any warranty. Promising is still more remote from the pure tort situation like a road accident between parties who had no previous dealings with one another. A motorist is no less liable for bad driving if he hangs L-plates on his car or, as is not uncommon, plasters on his rear window a notice drawing attention to his incompetence.

Promising, then, will not do as a general moral basis for objective liability in negligence. What of justified reliance? It is to this that Blackstone resorted to explain the doctor's liability for malpractice:[21]

> "For it hath been solemnly resolved that *mala praxis* is a great misdemeanour and offence at common law, whether it be for curiosity and experiment, or by neglect; because it breaks the trust which the party had placed in his physician, and tends to the patent's destruction."

But not every patient trusts his doctor. Some have doubts, but see no alternative. Nor do all motorists inspire the confidence of other road users. A car zigzags down the road towards me. I think the driver incompetent or drunk. But if by his bad driving he runs me down it is no defence to my action for damages that I did not think him competent. I rely on the competence of motorists in general, but need not suppose any particular motorist to be up to scratch in order to hold him to the objective standard.

In any case the crucial question is not whether in general people rely on others to meet the objective standard of competence but whether they are entitled to do so. In law they are, but on what moral basis? For the objective standard of competence imposes a form of strict liability on that minority of shortcomers who cannot attain it;

21. W. Blackstone, *Commentaries* (1st ed. 1769) vol. 3 p.122.

and to philosophers and many lawyers strict liability is a stumbling block. Nagel says that it "may have its legal uses but seems irrational as a moral position".[22]

2. Responsibility for Outcomes and Strict Liability

On the contrary, given certain conditions, strict liability can be morally defended. For present purposes liability is strict when it attaches to us by virtue of our conduct and its outcome alone, irrespective of fault.[23] It falls typically on those who pursue permissible but dangerous activities: storing explosives, running nuclear power stations, keeping wild animals, marketing drugs or other dangerous products, and, in France and Germany, driving a car. In common law systems an employer is strictly liable for the employee's torts in the course of employment, though it is also usually necessary to show that the employee is at fault. In such cases the law does not forbid people to undertake the activity or make the decision to employ Jones, because the activity or decision can have value. To forbid it would be illiberal. But society's consent is subject to the entrepreneur taking on himself, within certain limits, the risk that the decision or activity will misfire.[24]

The effect of strict liability is therefore to put an activity or decision at the risk of the agent or decision-maker as regards all but highly exceptional sequences of events. It does so irrespective of whether the persons storing the explosives, taking on Jones as foreman, or selling the dangerous drugs has taken reasonable care to see that what he does will not cause harm.

One point of imposing strict liability is to dispense with the need to prove fault on the part of people who are in fact at fault. If the activity that entails strict liability goes wrong, it generally goes wrong through someone's fault. But in some cases strict liability penalises

22. T. Nagel, "Moral Luck": *Mortal Questions* (1979) pp.24–38, at p.31.

23. Insurance is not on this definition a form of strict liability, since an insurer is not liable for the outcome of his own conduct.

24. The risk imposed on the entrepreneur does not normally extend to harm that would not have occurred in the absence of the dangerous activity or decision but that is attributable to *force majeure*, Act of God, and similar "external" causes.

not fault but bad luck, which in this context includes, besides ordinary accidents, the bad luck of being saddled with shortcomings.[25] The objective standard of liability in negligence has a like dual effect. Often it merely makes it easy to prove negligence on the part of someone who is in fact at fault. But sometimes it penalizes the bad luck of those who suffer from shortcomings. The principle involved in imposing ordinary strict liability, say for storing explosives, and in applying the objective standard of negligence is at bottom the same. Most of those held liable will be at fault but a minority will not. Thus in Britain a motorist who has an accident because, though he scraped through the test, he is too clumsy or stupid to drive properly can suffer, directly or through his insurer, for his bad luck. So under a different legal theory can his opposite number in France or Germany who is held liable for a road accident even though no fault on his part can be proved.

Holmes, in a classic passage of *The Common Law*, points to this combination of bad luck and blame. He says,

> "If a man is born hasty and awkward, is always having accidents and hurting himself or his neighbours, no doubt his congenital defects will be allowed for in the courts of Heaven, but his slips are no less troublesome to his neighbours than if they sprang from guilty neglect."

Hence

> "the law considers . . . what would be blameworthy in the average man, the man of ordinary intelligence and prudence, and determines liability by that. If we fall below the level in those gifts, it is our misfortune."

Holmes gives no morally convincing reason for holding the accident-prone man liable for his bad luck. The member of the awkward squad is not to blame for his defect. In the courts of Heaven, accordingly, he goes scot-free, but on earth his neighbours insist that he be held liable. True, but by what right? It is certainly bad luck to fall below a decent level in the gifts needed for social intercourse, but why should this misfortune entail legal liability?

Any principle that can justify responsibility for bad luck must be fair. If it is to be fair, it must entail that when we bear the risk of bad luck we also benefit if our luck is good. Allocation according to luck

25. Including "faults" of character and other shortcomings, which, viewed from a certain point of view, are the outcome of a cosmic lottery.

must cut both ways. So the system will be fair only if there are situations in which we implicitly bet on the outcomes of our actions.

Do such situations exist? Imagine that when we reach a decision to do X rather than Y – let us say to attempt a U-turn rather than to go on to the next roundabout – we are choosing to put our money on X and its outcome rather than Y and its outcome. When we opt for the U-turn rather than the roundabout, we implicitly bet that we will get to our destination quicker by making the U-turn. Our decision for U-turn rather than roundabout will be like a decision to put money on L'Escargot rather than Red Rum to win the Grand National. But we will not be like ordinary punters but rather jockeys who, contrary to existing practice, are allowed to back a horse and ride on it so that they can influence the result of their bet. Thus, when we choose X (say the U-turn), the bet we make is to be analysed as follows. We bet we can do X (the U-turn) and that X will have the more favourable outcome (getting there quicker). In calculating the odds for achieving the favourable outcome we have to discount the chance that we may not be able to do X or that the outcome of X, if we do it, will not be what we predict. Thus, we may not manage the U-turn; we may instead cause an accident. Or, we may manage it but find we were misinformed about the route, so that it would have been quicker to go on to the roundabout anyhow.

One difference between an implicit bet on outcomes and an ordinary wager concerns the stake and the winnings. In an ordinary bet we know the amount of the stake and often the potential winnings in advance. In implicit bets on the outcome of our actions, on the other hand, we do not precisely know the stake and winnings in advance; only that they will be proportionate to the outcome. The terms of the bets we make with other members of our community (and indirectly with ourselves) when we choose X rather than Y is that if we succeed and have guessed the outcome right we receive credit for it. If we manage the U-turn and get to our destination quicker we get credit for that success. But if we botch it, have an accident, or mistake the route, that is chalked up against us. This remains true even if the botch or miscalculation is not our fault, though of course it generally is. How much responsibility in terms of credit or debit accrues to us – how big the stake and winnings are – depends on how important the successful or botched outcome is in the eyes of others. We cannot tell the precise amounts in advance, but usually have a rough idea what they are likely to be. But whether the outcome is foreseeable or not, we can of course easily miscalculate. Despite the uncertainties, over a span of time more outcomes are likely to redound to our credit than to our debit, so that we are not permanently saddled with a losing ticket. Risk and benefit go hand in hand. *Ubi emolumentum ibi onus.*[26]

The betting system that I have outlined seems to me to correspond to our experience of everyday life. Our actions impinge on others, who resent it if the effects on them are harmful. So we are, unless indifferent to the reaction of others, forced to gamble in order to acquire credit and esteem and avoid exposure to discredit and resentment. Even by opting for inaction we cannot avoid putting out money on the table, because, as members of a community, we know that we will be held responsible for whatever good or ill we cause, including whatever harm our inaction produces in those cases where omissions count as causes. To choose and execute a course of conduct is to bet on your skill and judgement of the probabilities. Choosing is inescapably betting.

If this suggestion is correct, we live under a system by which a community allocates responsibility according to outcomes, and we are consequently forced to make bets on those outcomes. It is, I believe, no exaggeration to say that this dual system colours, often unconsciously, everything we do. Not only are actions and outcomes conventionally allocated to people but we and others are entitled to insist that they should be so allocated. Any moral or legal theory must therefore be condemned as inadequate unless it justifies the allocation of responsibility according to outcomes or shows that the system rests on a mistake.

Given certain conditions outcome allocation can be defended as fair. The necessary conditions are that the system must in its operation be impartial, reciprocal and over a period, beneficial. It must apply impartially to all those who possess a minimum capacity for reasoned choice and action. It must be reciprocal in that each such person is entitled to apply it to others and they to him. It must work so as to entitle each person to potential benefits that are likely on the whole to outweigh the detriments to which it subjects him. This makes it unfair to apply the system to the incapable, for whom there is no likely surplus of benefit

26. Justinian, *Institutes* 1.17; *Digest* 17.2.55; 50.17.10.

over detriment. But for the capable the three conditions are normally satisfied. All those who possess a minimum capacity stand to profit from the system of outcome allocation most of the time and, if there is a minority of permanent losers, they teeter on the edge of incapacity.[27]

The system of outcome allocation and outcome responsibility, which it entails, can therefore in certain conditions be defended as fair. Outcome responsibility automatically settles the bets made by people who by choosing a course of action implicitly put their money on the result. In any event outcome responsibility is, I contend, the basic type of responsibility in a community: more fundamental than either moral responsibility as generally understood, which requires fault, or legal responsibility, which requires either fault or special danger.

The analogy with a form of gambling in which we mostly win but sometime lose helps to explain and in part to justify not merely outcome responsibility but strict liability. In certain areas of life where there is a special risk that what we do will have a harmful outcome, society insists on pressing our responsibility for outcomes to its limits. Our fellow citizens insist that we pay up in terms of compensation rather than just apologise or ring for the ambulance or comfort the injured.

The justification of strict liability therefore depends in part on the fairness of outcome responsibility. Strict liability is one species of enhanced responsibility for outcomes. This does not entail that whenever a harmful outcome is properly allocated to someone, this justifies imposing on him a strict liability to compensate for that outcome. Contrary to what Epstein[28] and possibly Fletcher[29] at times seem to suggest, responsibility for a harmful outcome should not automatically involve a legal duty to compensate. An extra element is needed to ground the legal sanction. Sometimes the extra element is fault. Fault discloses a hostile or uncooperative disposition on the part of the harm doer, who either positively intends harm or disregards a known risk of it. For strict liability, the extra element is usually that the conduct of the harm doer carries with it a special risk of harm of the sort that has in fact come about. In that event, a conse-

27. We need to rethink the way in which to apply notions of responsibility to them, taking due account of their need to be seen as genuine persons.
28. R. Epstein, "A theory of strict liability": 2 *Journal of Legal Studies* (1973) 151.
29. G.P. Fletcher, "Fairness and utility in tort theory", *85 Harvard Law Rev.* (1972) 537.

quentialist argument for avoiding serious harm reinforces the non-consequentialist arguments for imposing outcome responsibility.

Legal theorists tend to ignore this combination because they view strict liability in isolation. They think of it as a burden imposed on a person who, not being provably at fault, should not morally be held responsible for the harm resulting from his conduct. But this is to overlook that outside the law people of full capacity stand to win more than they lose from the system of outcome allocation. We generally succeed in doing what we set about doing and get credit for it; only occasionally do we lose out. Of course the law of strict liability is solely concerned with the debit side of the account. It makes those who have incurred discredit pay compensation, even without fault. Yet in a wider perspective, strict liability when the shortcomer is not at fault, must be weighed not merely against a preponderance of successful outcomes, but against its obverse: the occasions on which by good luck our ill-judged actions have a happy outcome and we undeservedly escape discredit or even manage to obtain unmerited credit. Viewed in this light, strict liability merely serves to surcharge on grounds of social policy the debit side of an account that is in most instances comfortably in credit.

Though strict liability attaches when we choose a course of action to which special risks attach, that does not make it a species of fault liability. The person who chooses to pursue a dangerous activity may have good reasons for doing so; his conduct may in no way evince an objectionable attitude to others. He may not, when he decides to store explosives or employ Jones as foreman, appreciate the risks he is running. He may think the chances of fire negligible and Jones thoroughly competent. Does the fact that he may be strictly liable for a choice made in partial ignorance destroy the moral argument in favour of strict liability for risky activities? That depends.

Presumably a person should not be strictly liable if he did not understand the system by which in a society (1) people are held accountable for the good or bad outcomes of their actions and (2) a heavier potential liability attaches to dangerous activities than to relatively safe ones. Strict liability, like fault liability, should require the appropriate capacity. But there is a distinction between not understanding the system and not appreciating the risk involved in a particular choice, for example to employ Jones or store explosives.

Strict liability and fault liability run parallel in this respect. Those who do not understand outcome allocation and the difference between right and wrong (or lawful and unlawful) are generally held incapable of fault, but in order to be guilty of fault they need not know that a particular action is wrongful. On this analysis, virtually everyone who possesses the general capacity needed for outcome responsibility also possesses the capacity to be legally responsible both on the basis of fault and strict liability.

A further point that bears on the fairness of outcome allocation, and so of strict liability, is that neither is something that the person subject to them has chosen. Does that make these institutions morally dubious? We have never made a social contract providing for outcome allocation, still less for strict liability. They bind us willy-nilly.

It is true that we have no choice in the matter. But outcome allocation can be defended on grounds deeper than the overall balance of benefit over burden; and so, in its wake, can strict liability. For outcome allocation is crucial to our identity as persons; and, unless we were persons who possessed an identity, the question of whether it was fair to subject us to responsibility could not arise. If actions and outcomes were not ascribed to us on the basis of our bodily movements and their mental accompaniments, we could have no continuing history or character.[30] There would indeed be bodies and, associated with them, minds. Each would posses a certain continuity. They could be labelled A, B, C. But having decided nothing and done nothing these entities would hardly be people.

In the real world, fortunately, human bodily movements and their mental accompaniments are with some exceptions interpreted as actions and decisions. They are ascribed to authors, who accordingly count as persons; and it is by virtue of these ascriptions that each of us has a history, an identity and a character. But there is a price to be paid for being a person. As the counterpart of this status we are responsible for our actions and their consequences, and sometimes this responsibility exposes us to legal sanctions. To ascribe personhood and responsibility to people in this way is to apply normative principles. It is not merely that others attribute to us an identity and a character, but that we are entitled to claim them for ourselves and

30. H.L.A. Hart and T. Honoré, *Causation in the Law* (2nd ed. 1985) lxxx–lxxxi.

to ascribe them to others. Others in turn not only hold us responsible for our actions and their outcomes, but are entitled to do so. Of course the balance between personhood and responsibility cannot, any more than the system of outcome allocation, be said to rest on a social contract. We have never decided to assume responsibility in exchange for the gift of personal identity. Both are natural in the sense that we can neither choose them nor give them up.[31] Considered as a bargain, the exchange would not even, properly speaking, be in our interest; for to be responsible is part of what it means to be a person and hence to have interests. But the normative principles involved may be regarded in a pre-moral sense as well-founded, since they embody a balance between identity and responsibility.

Such are the normative arguments for allocation according to outcome and, as a corollary, for strict legal liability for the harmful upshot of risky conduct. In practice most ordinary people endorse the former and most lawyers the latter, though either might be hard put to say why. Virtually no one inside or outside the law believes that fault and desert are the sole basis of responsibility.[32] In their off-duty moments even those philosophers and theologians who in theory cleave to fault alone assign credit and discredit for actions and their outcomes in cases where blame and praise are not in point. Take a non-moral example: the contrasting fortunes of X and Y, two footballers playing in a needle match. X miskicks but a gust of wind carries the ball into the opposing goal. He is credited with a goal, but not praised for scoring it. It would be better, of course, had he been skilful as well as lucky, for he would then both be credited with the goal and praised for scoring it. Y aims a skilful shot at goal, but this time a gust of wind diverts it. He is praised for his good shot but not credited with a goal. It would be still worse for him had his shot been a bad one. X is lucky, Y unlucky; but it is the outcome of their actions, not what they deserve, that primarily determines credit or its absence. Desert merely increases or diminishes credit or discredit. Take a legal example. I fire at my rival intending to kill him. It would be murder if I succeeded, but I miss. I am guilty only of an attempt. If fault is to be judged by disposition my fault is as great as if I had hit him, but my responsibility is less. Now for an extra-legal example. If purely by

31. Cf. P. Strawson, 48 *Proceedings of the British Academy* (1962) 1, 24 (on induction).
32. "Forgive us our sins both voluntary and involuntary" (Orthodox liturgy).

your fault in darting out into the road I run you over, I must stop, send for the ambulance and give you what help I can in the meantime. My responsibility is not as great as if I had been at fault. It may not be legal: that depends on the applicable system of law. It may not be moral in the sense that I am morally responsible for the accident itself. But, just because I have hurt you, I am responsible, and by virtue of that responsibility bound to take certain steps. Indeed, unless I am wholly insensitive, I shall feel and express regret for the harm I have done. For it is a myth that fault and desert are essential to responsibility. They serve rather to increase the credit or discredit for the outcome of our behaviour that we incur in any event.

It is only this primary outcome responsibility that can explain why we (rightly) judge murder more severely than attempted murder and causing death by dangerous driving more severely than dangerous driving. It is said that morally the harmful outcome makes no difference; and indeed the difference between causing death by dangerous driving and mere dangerous driving, like the difference between aiming a good shot at goal and scoring a goal, is causal, a matter of outcomes. On a narrow view of morality the cases are not morally distinguishable. For allocation according to outcomes is not allocation to according to effort, talent or disposition. A good outcome can sometimes be achieved with less effort than a bad outcome, and by a person with less talent and a worse character. Outcome allocation is allocation according to results, whether they constitute achievements or botches. But it does not follow that the system of allocation according to result, in contrast with its application to individual instances, lacks a moral or pre-moral basis. The person concerned, though he cannot be sure what the outcome of his action will be, has chosen to act in the knowledge that he will be credited or debited with whatever it turns out to be. Moreover, we cannot opt out of the system by which we obtain credit for favourable outcomes; and so we cannot slough off the burden of discredit either. Finally, it is outcomes that in the long run make us what we are.

3. Capacity and Freedom

It seems possible, then, to justify both outcome responsibility and the liability, strict or fault based, that legal systems superimpose on it, if those held responsible have the proper capacity and make the relevant choice. To be outcome responsible they must understand both the system of allocation according to outcomes and how in practice to use causal notions to settle what counts as the outcome of an action. The relevant choice is to choose to act knowing that the outcome of the action will be attributed to the agent.

To be responsible for fault, morally or legally, the person concerned must in addition understand right and wrong (or lawful and unlawful) and the system of allocation based on that. The relevant choice is the decision to act, in the knowledge of how that distinction is employed, either with a view to doing harm or in disregard of a known risk of harm. To have the capacity for strict liability the person must understand that a special responsibility attaches to socially dangerous activities. The relevant choice is the decision in the light of that knowledge to embark on the activity in question.

Thus explained, the two forms of legal liability are seen to be species of the genus outcome responsibility. The main difference between them is that when someone is at fault he should by standards known to him have acted differently, whereas when he is held to strict liability this need not be the case. But the fact that the person held liable has violated a known standard, though it may increase his responsibility, does not create it.

But is it not a condition of every form of responsibility that the person responsible could have acted differently? The capacities so far listed have been cognitive: the ability to understand cause and consequence, right and wrong, the notion of a dangerous activity, and the systems of allocating responsibility based on these factors. Since choice is admittedly a condition of responsibility, does it not follow that the person held responsible must also possess the cognitive capacity to choose and to control his conduct in accordance with his choice?

The capacity to reach decisions and act on them must on any view be a condition of responsibility. But how are we to fix what precise capacity is needed and test its presence on a given occasion? Intuitively we think of ourselves, in one mood, as responsible for an outcome only when we could have done something different that would have brought about a different outcome. Philosophers and lawyers have without great success debated how to analyse this capacity.[33] In a different mood, however, we are prepared to bypass the supposed capacity to do otherwise. In that alternative mood we think of ourselves as responsible even when our conduct is determined by internal factors such as limited intelligence or bad temper that are, either in the short or long run, beyond our control. These internal factors, unlike external constraints, do not then seem to relieve us of responsibility. Yet we cannot, at any rate when in their grip, do otherwise. So we catch ourselves believing, perhaps not at one and the same moment, that the ability to do otherwise both is and is not a condition of responsibility.[34] That is unacceptable. If we find ourselves embracing contradictory beliefs, it is time to abandon or modify one of them.

The need to do this, and a hint of the best way to set about it, emerges if we reflect on how lawyers have tried to solve puzzles about the capacity of children. What standard of care does the law of negligence expect of a child who crosses a busy street or plays a game with a stick? It seems attractive to opt, not for an adult standard, nor a uniform standard for all children, but for whatever standard the particular child is capable of. But how can we discover what this is? How are we to judge, say, the capacity of a child of eight who knows that he must take care not to put his companion's eye out with a stick, but is in the excitement of the game bad at keeping the danger in mind? Was he at that moment capable of thinking about his playmate's eye and acting accordingly? Even supposing that in the excitement of the game the average child of eight remains careful to avoid poking his friend's eye out, perhaps this particular child is immature for his age. So in setting the standard for children, some jurisdictions lay down that account must be taken not only of the child's age but of his experience and maturity.[35] Assume, then, that most children of the experience and maturity of this child would have avoided putting their friend's eye out. That still does not show that this child could have

33. E.g. B. Aune, 27 *Analysis* (1967) pp.191–5; K. Lehrer, 29 *Analysis* (1968) pp.29–32.
34. The oscillation is forcefully brought out by T. Nagel, *The View from Nowhere* (1986) ch.7.
35. E.g. *Mack* v. *Davis* 76 Ill. App 2d 88, 221 NE 2d 121,126 (1966): age, experience and intelligence.

avoided the accident if "could have avoided" refers to a capacity exercisable in all the conditions of the incident. For this child, relatively mature though he was, may have been distracted at the crucial moment by, say, a sudden shout, that would not have distracted an average child of the same maturity. Do we then go on to ask whether the average child of the same age, experience and maturity who was distracted by a shout would have put his playmate's eye out? Nor is there any good reason to stop there. We can go on to add detail upon detail. But as the required standard moves asymptotically towards that of the particular child in all the concrete conditions of the case, it ceases to be a standard and becomes an ever more detailed description of the untoward event.

What this example rawly exposes is that the question whether the child was "capable" of doing otherwise, and so was responsible, is not a plain question of fact. Knowing more about the child does not settle the answer. On the contrary, what we need to know in order to determine responsibility is whether a child of a certain degree of, say, maturity is expected to behave with that degree of maturity, not in the sense that he will predictably behave in that way on a given occasion, but that he takes the risk of behaviour that displays a lesser degree of maturity.[36] And while it is no accident that the word "expected" lends itself to both a descriptive and a normative interpretation, the question "what is to be expected of him?" is meant to combine elements of both. The usual behaviour of the child or similar children bears on the answer but does not determine it. A child who in general possesses a certain degree of maturity does not on every occasion display that maturity; and it is a gratuitous assumption that he *could* do so. Hence if a child's general level of maturity determines what law or morality requires of him, that is because we think it fair to judge him by the standard that he usually manages to attain. But even if we adopt this so-called "subjective" standard, really intermediate between the objective and the subjective, we still impose on the child the risk that in a particular instance he may not come up to it and may in the special conditions of the case be unable to do so.

Does it follow that we have to abandon "capacity to act otherwise" as a condition of responsibility? No, for we can give it a more plausi-

36. Esser-Schmidt, *Schuldrecht* (6th ed. 1984) vol. I p.377: the object of the law of obligations is to divide zones of risk from one another.

ble interpretation. The capacity to act otherwise has hitherto been taken to be a capacity exercisable *in the particular circumstances in which the person concerned finds himself.* Legal statements of the objective standard of care, for example, all refer to the care to be expected of a model person in the circumstances. None set a standard to be complied with regardless.

The word "circumstance" invites a distinction between external and internal factors.[37] The most obvious circumstances are things outside us, such as place, time, weather, noise, social pressure. The person involved (let us call him or her the agent) must take account of them in deciding what to do but is not expected to change them. He is not responsible for them, for they are not part of his being, but part of the scene on which he has to act. The most obvious factors that are not circumstances are things that are inside the agent or part of his makeup, like being stupid or in a bad temper. The person concerned must either overcome these or face the consequences that ensue. It follows that what counts as a circumstance is often not determined by crude geography, inside or outside. It can be a normative question: is it good policy to treat such-and-such a factor, let us say inexperience, as something for which the person concerned is responsible? Thus, there is a case for treating some aspects of a person's physical makeup, though in one sense internal to him, as circumstances of which he must take account but which he cannot be expected to alter. Someone who is too short to see over a wall must take account of his disability by walking round the side or, if that is not possible, fetching a ladder.[38] He is not to be treated as if he could see over the wall unaided.

But the process of externalising the elements that go into a person's makeup cannot be carried beyond a certain point without obliterating the distinction between internal factors for which a person is responsible and circumstances for which he is not. The boundary can shift but it cannot be wiped out without eliminating the person along with the responsibility.[39] For given the totality of internal factors – the person's makeup and his physical, mental and emotional state at

37. H. and L. Mazeaud and A. Tunc, above n.15, vol. 1 s.431.
38. Cf. *Mahan* v. *State to Use of Carr,* 172 Md. 373, 191 Atl. 575, 579–80 (1937); and for deafness *Otterbeck* v. *Lamb* 85 Nev. 456, 456 Pac. 2d 855 (1969).
39. "Dans la vie sociale on répond de son être": Mazeaud and Tunc, above n.15, vol. I p.490.

the time and place in question – it is implausible to suppose that on a given occasion he can act otherwise than he does. If I am in a filthy temper I cannot at the same time conform to a model of calm deliberation. If to be responsible the person concerned must have been able to act otherwise in the circumstances, then not all internal factors can count as circumstances.

Legal systems recognise this. Though they vary in what they regard as internal factors in relation to which the actor is at risk, all agree that he should be saddled with some such factors that are not, therefore, to be accounted circumstances. Thus, everyone must bear the risk of his own bad temper or irritability; but it is disputed whether inexperience is to be treated as a circumstance rather than a deficiency for which the inexperienced person must take the rap.[40] If a surgeon is sued for negligence is it relevant that he is newly qualified and has not performed the operation before? The issue is a normative one on which opinions legitimately differ.[41]

Though there is often doubt where best to draw the line between internal factors and circumstances, both our everyday judgements and the law of negligence assume that it must be drawn somewhere. A driver must drive reasonably in the circumstances, where circumstances include the slippery road and the dim light but not fatigue or a lapse of concentration. But why is a lapse of concentration not accounted a circumstance? Could one not argue that a driver whose concentration lapses need only conform to the model of a driver, otherwise competent, whose concentration has lapsed? Why is the unfortunate driver blamed for his lapse and held to be negligent in law? Every driver has some lapses of concentration.

To put it generally, in no activity or walk of life can people consistently maintain the high standard of skill and care required by law without variation. Indeed that is to understate the matter. Empirical studies show, for example, a high rate of error on the part of even competent drivers.[42] It is not only the stupid and clumsy who are

40. Above n.2.

41. On the view taken here it is not unfair to hold the inexperienced surgeon, etc., to the standard of an experienced surgeon. He can in the normal course of events look forward to a much longer period of professional practice, after he has gained the necessary experience, than the relatively short period spent acquiring it, so that, taking his professional practice as a whole, he is likely to be an overall winner.

42. U.S. Department of Transportation: *Automobile Insurance and Compensation Study* 1970 pp.177–8: "In Washington D.C. a 'good' driver viz. one without an accident

incapable of meeting the objective standard of care on the road. The intelligent and adroit cannot consistently meet it either. So if a vigilant and skilful driver has a lapse of attention from which an accident results, and we say that, unlike the driver with slow reactions, he could have swerved in time, our ground for saying this cannot be a supposed capacity to remain alert every moment that he is at the wheel. We must instead be thinking of his general capacity as a driver. To ascribe responsibility to a competent driver whose attention has lapsed we need not believe that given all the elements internal and external of the concrete situation he could, despite his lapse, have swerved and avoided the accident.

If then it is a condition of responsibility that the person to be held responsible could have acted differently in the circumstances, circumstances must be distinguished from those internal factors for which the agent is on normative grounds to be held at risk. We then have a choice. Either we abandon the notion that responsibility depends on the ability to do otherwise in the circumstances. Or we retain the notion, but construe the required capacity as a *general* ability to perform the sort of action that would in the instant case have led to a different outcome. This general ability need not have been exercisable in all the concrete conditions, external and internal, of the case.

The second view is preferable since it enables us to retain in modified form our common sense belief in the importance of capacity to act otherwise as an element in responsibility. On this view the capacity to remain alert, when alertness would have avoided the accident, does not refer to the possibility of someone's remaining in a steady state of alertness for an indefinite period but rather to an ability to remain alert in normal conditions most of the time. So, though we are responsible for lack of alertness, it is not a condition of our responsibility that we should be able to exercise our capacity to remain alert on every occasion when it is sought to hold us responsible. To construe capacity in this way as general capacity is not to embrace determinism as a world view, but to make the point that, if law and morals require for responsibility an invariant capacity that can be exercised on every occasion, no one will consistently be responsible for his conduct.

---

within the preceding five years commits on average, in five minutes of driving, at least nine errors of different kinds."

That is not an acceptable conclusion. Moreover, we are not driven to it. We can take the view that, even if human conduct is determined by the factors, internal and external, present on a given occasion – which we have at present no way of deciding – an agent can properly be judged on the basis of his general capacity.

The analysis of capacity here advocated is not new. I put it forward more than twenty years ago.[43] The theme of my paper, in the idiom of the age, was the distinction between "can general" and "can particular". A golfer can (general) hole a six-foot putt if he possesses the general capacity to do so; and he possesses that capacity if it is usually the case that when he tries he succeeds. It is compatible with his possessing this general capacity that on a given occasion he cannot (particular) hole a putt of six feet or less. If he tries to hole a particular putt and does not succeed that shows that he could not (particular) do so. It will nevertheless be true that he could (general) have holed it, since he possessed the resources physical and mental to succeed. But internal factors, such as fatigue or lack of concentration, may have prevented him exercising his capacities on this occasion.

Though reflected in verbal usage, the point is normative rather than linguistic. The reason for allotting responsibility to people on the basis of their general capacity is that they then stand to win most of the time, because it is true by definition that, when they try, they usually perform up to their ability. It is for this reason that in many contexts we rightly insist in both law and morals on fault as a condition of responsibility. The fault system penalises those whose conduct displays a bad disposition, but at the same time affords people fair opportunities of escaping sanctions for botches and bad outcomes most of the time. It provides an incentive, often internal as well as external, to take advantage of these opportunities. Therein lies its justification, not in the unfounded assumption that, given the external and internal constraints present on a given occasion, the person at fault could (particular) have done otherwise than he did.

Thus to judge people according to their general capacity neither rules out nor requires determinism. General capacities can be measured by how people generally perform when they try to execute a given type of action, like shutting the door or crossing the street or

43. "Can and Can't", 73 *Mind* (1964) 463–479, reprinted, below p.144. Endorsed by D. Dennett, *Elbow Room* (1984) pp.147–8.

holing a six-foot putt. Whether their choices and performances are determined by pre-existing factors has no obvious bearing on the fairness of judging them on this basis. But such judgements sit most comfortably with the view that, while strict determinism may be false, a person's character, aims and general capacity plus the circumstances of which he is aware normally determine his choice; his choice normally determines his conduct; and his conduct plus the circumstances in which he acts normally determine the outcome. If we are to be responsible for the outcomes of our actions, we are likely to find these loosely framed hypotheses reassuring rather than alarming. How else would we be able to act in accordance with our character and general capacities or to achieve our aims, including the reflexive aim of changing, to a limited extent, our own character and capacities?

Even if our conduct is incompletely determined, the freedom we value is independent of this indeterminacy. Freedom is, in this context, a notion partly descriptive and partly normative. External or (better) circumstantial freedom depends on the absence of oppressive constraints that result in our conduct failing to reflect our character and aims. Conduct in the face of such oppressive constraints is not rated as fully voluntary, and our responsibility for it is correspondingly diminished. That we are unfree and so not the true authors of actions undertaken in conditions of oppressive constraint is plainly a normative notion, though it presupposes a certain descriptive background. It is the same with the internal aspects of freedom. Our internal freedom is circumscribed by our general capacities for understanding and action. That people who possess adequate general capacities are the authors and originating cause of their conduct and its outcome is, once again, a normative conception that presupposes a certain descriptive background. We are, consistently with this notion, specially free when the conduct and its outcome lies within our specific capacities, so that we can plan to bring about the outcome with some confidence. Actions undertaken in these conditions afford the prime example of fully voluntary conduct.

4. Conclusion

The argument has been complex but its core is simple. Our responsibility for what we do and for its outcome is inseparable from our status as persons. We cannot disclaim outcome responsibility without undermining that status; and outcome responsibility is therefore more fundamental than moral and legal responsibility, which are species of it. But the fairness of holding someone responsible outside or inside the law depends on their possessing a general capacity for decision and action such that, under the system of bets into which society forces them, they stand over a span of time to win more than they lose. The system is not a fair one to apply to those whose limited capacities make them consistent losers. Given a sufficient general capacity, however, it involves no great extension of principle for the law to impose strict liability for risky activities alongside fault liability for conduct that discloses an uncooperative disposition. To bear the risk of bad luck is inseparable from being a choosing person.

3

ARE OMISSIONS LESS CULPABLE[1]?

1. Introduction

In 1977 Jonathan Glover published a powerful attack on the "acts-and-omissions doctrine".[2] The doctrine, in his words, holds that in certain contexts failure to perform an act, with foreseen bad consequences of that failure, is morally less bad than to perform a different act that has the identical bad consequences. Harmful omissions are sometimes less culpable than equally harmful acts. Glover denied this and other philosophers have likewise argued that, other things being equal, there is no moral difference between killing and letting die,[3] or between positive and negative instrumentality.[4]

Other things are usually not equal. One who poisons food sent to starving refugees is likely to kill some of them, will cause great resentment, and is a constant menace to others. One who fails to contribute to the refugees' relief fund is not certain to bring about anyone's death, since others may provide the food. His conduct may be criticised but will not be widely resented, even if he does not care whether the refugees survive. His character is probably little worse than average. But examples can be devised in which these differences are ironed out. It then becomes much less obvious that doing harm is worse than omission to help.

My reason for discussing the acts-and-omissions doctrine afresh is that, though law is strongly committed to it, lawyers have not been very successful in finding a rationale for it. The most plausible arguments for sanctioning acts more severely than omissions have so far

1. First published in *Essays for Patrick Atiyah* (ed. Peter Cane and Jane Stapleton 1991) pp.31–52.
2. J. Glover, *Causing Death and Saving Lives* (1977) ch.7.
3. H.M. Malm, "Killing, letting die and simple conflicts" [hereafter *Killing*] 18 *Philosophy and Public Affairs* (1989) 238, 253.
4. The phrase is used by J. Bennett, "Morality and Consequences" [hereafter *Morality*]: 11 *Tanner Lectures* (1981) 47, 72.

been economic. One can refrain from a great many harmful acts, like poisoning, at the same time, while it is difficult or impossible to combine more than one helpful act, like providing food.[5] The benefit of abstention is also widely distributed, in that if I abstain from doing harm no one is harmed, while the benefit of helpful acts is confined to the few who get the food that I can provide. So it imposes a lighter burden on the person concerned, with a more widely distributed benefit to others, to make him abstain from harmful acts than to oblige him to do helpful ones. To require a positive act normally imposes a greater cost in time, effort, skill and money than a prohibition with similar results.[6] In a society in which most people see to their own subsistence it involves a cost to transfer this responsibility to another. No such transfer cost is involved in requiring everyone to refrain from harming others.

These are some of the arguments that tend to show that it is on the whole cheaper for society to protect life and health by forbidding harm-doing than by requiring people to help others. It also costs less to distribute the burdensome positive duties so that no one has to undertake more than a limited number of them, and that those are preferably of the sort that they would be inclined to undertake anyhow. It is cost-effective (including psychological costs) for parents to look after their own children and only in special circumstances other people's.

If we assume that it is morally worse, because more selfish, to refuse to incur a small cost in the interest of others than a large expense, it follows that it is usually worse to do harm than to fail to help. It is also worse to fail to help those whom one is naturally inclined to help than to fail to help others. Whatever the force of these arguments, societies in practice adopt the acts-and-omissions theory, even when they have sophisticated welfare systems. In both criminal and tort law, liability for an omission is exceptional. In the language of duty, which is central to legal thinking, there is liability for omission only when one can show the breach of a duty to act owed to some individual or to the state, over and above the (mainly negative) duties we all owe one another as fellow human beings.

But it does not follow from the fact that it is cheaper to regulate society mainly by forbidding harmful acts that these acts are morally

---

5. Bennett, *Morality*, above n.4, at p.87.
6. Not always: see Section 4 below.

worse than omissions, apart from the fact that it costs little to abstain from them. If it turns out that, apart from considerations of cost, not contributing to the relief fund is morally just as bad, or almost as bad, as poisoning the relief food, we shall have to ask whether law and conventional morality are justified in making so sharp a distinction between acts and omissions on the basis of cost alone.

I shall argue that, when conduct is judged from the standpoint of responsibility for the harm it brings about, the acts-and-omissions doctrine is broadly sound. Nothing will be said about the relative culpability of acts and omissions apart from their consequences, or of acts and omissions that violate social convention rather than morality or law. Rude conduct is often judged according to the distress it creates; and one can ask whether positive discourtesy (making a rude gesture) is on a par with negative discourtesy (cutting someone in the street) if the distress caused is similar. The answer – if it is possible to give one in general terms – must await another occasion.

Since writers use slightly different terms in discussing omissions, it is as well to explain at the outset how the term is used in this essay. Conduct can be divided into doing and non-doing. Sometimes conduct is contrary to a norm. A doing contrary to a norm is a commission, a not-doing an omission. Omissions are therefore those not-doings that violate norms. Norms are divided for this purpose into ordinary norms and norms that impose distinct duties, a concept that will be explained shortly. Omissions that violate distinct duties may be termed distinct omissions.

Positive acts, I contend, are often worse than omissions that violate ordinary norms, because they create the primary harms and risks of harm that omissions fail to remedy. But on the "distinct duties" theory, omissions that violate distinct duties are usually on a level with positive acts that violate these duties. The distinct duties theory holds that we have, besides the background duties that we owe to all, distinct duties to other people and associations, including the state, that vary from person to person according to individual circumstance and past dealings between them. Examples are the duties of parents to children, of citizens to the state, of those who endanger others to the persons endangered, and of those who can rescue others in an emergency to the victims. How these distinct duties are thought to come into being is discussed in Section 3.

If the distinct duties theory is right, positive acts are on a level, or nearly on a level, with omissions in contexts where the person concerned – the agent as he may be called – is under a distinct duty like that of parent to child. It then makes little or no difference whether the agent breaks his duty by a positive act or an omission. Beating and starving one's child are equally culpable when the harm to the child is equal (say, comparable suffering culminating in death). They are equal because the distinct duty counteracts the otherwise greater significance of positive acts by requiring the person subject to it to devote time, trouble, or money to fulfilling the duty, and in that way eliminate or reduce the moral significance of the cost difference. On the distinct duty theory, distinct duties are stronger than the background duties we owe to everyone and take priority over them. Moreover, distinct duties can have varying strengths among themselves. Though both the parent and the householder have distinct duties, a parent's duty to a child may be stronger than a householder's to a visitor. It may have a higher priority and require more of the person subject to it.

But when background duties are in issue, positive acts are normally worse than omissions. Background duties are indeed largely (though not exclusively) duties to abstain from doing harm or creating an unjustified risk of harm. Beating someone else's child and not feeding it are not on a level, even if the harm to the child is the same (I may know that some child will suffer if I do not contribute to a relief-fund just as much as it would from a beating). Even if one has some background duty to care for other children, it is a weaker duty than that of caring for children who are dependent on one. So beating that other child is worse than not giving money to feed it.

The distinct duties theory attracts lawyers and also philosophers who attach weight to rights and obligations. Other philosophers reject the theory, and give little weight to talk of duties. Utilitarians and other consequentialists think not merely that conduct should be commended and judged by its likely outcome, but that the consequences to everyone should count. On some theories, the welfare and so forth of each person counts equally and must be added up (maximizing theories); on others the less-well-off count for more (distributive theories). Let us call these theories in which an agent's duty is to produce the best overall result, whether the best is the maximum or the best-distributed, "optimizing theories". Optimizing theories make redundant the notion of duties owed to particular individuals or bodies. According to them, for example, that parents should look after their children counts not as a duty but at most as a rule of thumb, arrived at on the basis that if they do so, that is likely on the whole to optimize overall happiness or welfare, or that it is too costly to get people to abandon their natural commitments even for something that is in principle better.

On optimising theories there is no intrinsic moral difference between acts and omissions. One must behave so as to bring about the optimum good, for example, the optimum overall welfare. The best (and hence the right) way of doing this may sometimes be by abstaining from action and sometimes by a positive act. There can be no systematic preference for the one over the other, but at most a rough indication based on a rule of thumb. It follows that it cannot in any systematic way be more culpable to fail to optimize welfare or satisfaction by a positive intervention than by an abstention. When the resulting shortfall from the optimum is the same, and the cost of refraining or doing is similar, acts and omissions must be equally bad. The optimising theories, therefore, lead to a different conclusion about the relative culpability of acts and omissions from the distinct duties theory.

The discussion that follows is intended to defend the acts-and-omissions doctrine, at least in certain contexts, and to show the connection between it, the notion of intervention, and the distinct duties theory.

I believe my enterprise is appropriate to a volume in honour of Patrick Atiyah. It has indirectly a bearing on his theory of contract, an aspect of his work that has rightly been seen as original and challenging. At times Atiyah argues that to make a promise is no more than to admit or fix the extent of a duty based on some other ground, such as benefit or reliance.[7] On this view, promises are no more than evidence, sometimes conclusive evidence, of the promisor's obligation. In other passages Atiyah seems to allow some independent weight to promising, but treats not keeping a promise as a rather trivial default, unless the making of the promise induced the promisee to rely on its being kept and so to incur expense or forego opportunities.[8]

7. P.S. Atiyah, *Promises, Morals and Law* (Oxford 1981) ch.7
8. Atiyah's third head of liability in this area, benefit, usefully reminds us that responsibility need not be based on the conduct of the person held responsible. A person can

Not keeping a promise counts as an omission (Section 2) for which on the distinct-duties theory (Section 3) the promisor is liable by virtue of the positive act of making a promise. But the duty to keep the promise may rest on more than one ground. The promise may merely create an expectation in the promisee that it will be kept; or it may induce him to incur loss by reliance on the promise. If the promise is not kept, the promisee is in the first case no better off than before, but in the second is actually worse off. It is presumably worse to make the promisee worse off than not to make him better off. People resent having their position made worse more than not having it improved as they expected, though in monetary terms the shortfall may be the same. Harm is worse than disappointment; compare a wage-cut with the refusal of an increase. The contrast, as explained further in Section 3 A and E, depends on the differing grounds of the duty to keep the promise in the two cases: creating a risk of harm and giving an undertaking respectively. This difference has some bearing on the reasons for holding acts to be in general worse than omissions that bring about the same harm (Section 4).

My plan of campaign will be as follows. Some logical groundwork is first called for (Section 2). The next stage (Section 3) is to analyse the reasons for imposing distinct duties, by which people often have a duty positively to intervene in the interest, individual or collective, of others. The final part (Section 4) seeks to assess the relative culpability of acts and omissions, something that is easier once account is taken of the social context of the conduct in question.

2. Positive Acts, Not-doings, Omissions

"If a child is neglected, it is not only his father who omits to look after him; everyone else omits to look after him also", says Glanville Williams.[9] That is plainly wrong, and violates ordinary usage, which here marks a useful distinction. Only those parents, relatives, foster-

---

be responsible not because of what he did or did not do but because of a benefit received or, more widely, because of his position in society. It is not true (Bennett, *Morality*, above n.4, at pp.476–9) that "because he did" and "because he did not" are exhaustive of prima facie responsibility (Section 3.D below).

9. *Criminal Law: The General Part* (2nd ed., London 1961) p.4.

parents, managers of a children's home, baby-sitters, and so on who are charged with looking after the child can be said to omit to do so. "Omit" is both a normative and a pejorative term. An omission is not-doing-something, but not every not-doing-something is an omission. To omit implies that one ought to have done what was not done.[10] Often the "ought" is legal or moral, as in the case of the neglected child, but it need not be. Apart from omitting to look after a child in one's charge one can omit or forget or leave out the bicarbonate of soda in the cake recipe. I can fail to take a coat when it would be wise to do so because cold weather is expected, and neglect to shake hands when shaking hands would be polite. In these informal contexts we often speak of failing or neglecting rather than omitting, "omit" being a rather formal equivalent of the other terms. In sum, one can omit to do something only when, for whatever reason, the situation calls for it to be done.

The "ought" that is needed to turn not-doing-something into an omission to do it can be a simple matter of prudence, courtesy, or conformity to a rule or recipe. On the other hand, a person who changes his habits does not merely by doing so omit to do what he did previously. The tippler who usually goes to the Fox and Hounds for a drink at six-thirty does not omit to do so if one day he decides to stay at home. He does not go to the inn; but, unless he has promised or is required by ties of friendship to be there, he does not omit to go there. The mere fact that he knows that someone will rely on his presence may give rise to a duty to warn the person concerned that he will not be there. In that case he will be open to criticism for omitting to give the warning rather than omitting to be present.

An omission violates a norm. Omissions therefore entail responsibility, but at times this is of the minor sort involved in being forgetful, imprudent, or impolite rather than legally or morally at fault. It is the sort of responsibility that often calls for nothing more than an apology. On other occasions – and there is no very clear borderline – omissions are legally and/or morally significant. They are so when the norm violated is legal or moral, but not otherwise. In law this point is expressed by saying that an omission is legally significant only if there is a legal duty to act. This raises the question, to which we must

10. E. Weinrib, "Omissions and Responsibility", *Phil. Quart.* 30 (1980) 1. Cf. Bennett, *Morality*, above n.4, at p.50.

return in Section 3, of the sort of reason that can give rise to a moral or legal duty to act.

But there is more to the analysis of omissions than the fact that they must be contrary to some norm. An omission is a species of not-doing, of negative conduct, by which I mean conduct that is in its relevant aspect negative, an instance of negative instrumentality.[11] In analysing omissions we cannot avoid an inquiry into the difference between doing and not-doing. The inquiry should aim at a distinction between doing and not-doing, between positive and negative conduct, that is morally and normatively neutral. Otherwise the answer to the question whether harm-causing omissions are less culpable than positive acts will be built into the definition.

There is, however, in my view a limit to the neutrality that can be achieved. In particular, it is a mistake to think that by finding a normatively neutral distinction between acts and omissions, it will be possible to show that utilitarianism or some other optimizing theory, according to which there is no moral distinction between the two, is correct. If a distinction such as that between doing and not-doing is prominently marked in thought and language it is sure to mark a difference in social evaluation too, and that difference is not likely to be arbitrary.

Let us, for convenience, call the person whose conduct is in question the agent, whether the agent's conduct was positive or negative. Not-doing-something is not an easy notion to analyse. Strictly speaking, conduct itself cannot be negative, since only phrases and propositions are negative. Conduct can of course be described by a proposition that contains a negative, as in "James did not stop speaking", but that does not settle that James's conduct was negative, for one could convey the same sense by saying "he went on speaking". The point of "he did not stop speaking" is likely to be that James was expected to stop but did not. The alternative, positive way of putting it does not carry the same implication, or not so strongly. But whichever form is used refers to the same flow of words on James's part.

Clearly what is at stake in the contrast of doing and not-doing must be to do with the behaviour itself and not merely with the way in which it is described. Corresponding to every positive description of

11. The phrase is Bennett's.

conduct there is an equivalent negative one: shooting is equivalent to not refraining from shooting. The converse is not true, at any rate not in a straightforward way. There is no positive expression that means the same as not going to the cinema. One could if necessary invent the (positive) verb to "discinematize" to express the idea ("she decided to discinematize and concentrate on her work").

So it is possible, if not always natural, to describe conduct with positive and negative expressions that have the same meaning. Apart from this point about the resources of language, the same conduct can be described in an indefinite number of ways that have different meanings. Some of these would naturally be put in a positive form, others negatively. We can say of a motorist who drove at 90 mph that he did not drive at 70 or 110 or any speed other than 90 mph. Sometimes there is point in the negative expression (for example, if the speed limit is 70 mph, or most motorists drive at that speed). But most of the possible negative descriptions of conduct will sound unnatural and will be pointless. Whatever the agent's conduct, the list of negative propositions describing it – the list of things the person did not do on that occasion – will outstrip the list of possible positive descriptions. But the list of things a person was not doing at a given moment is endless and, shorn of a special rhetorical point,[12] boring.

To whittle down the list of propositions describing conduct, the first step is to eliminate those that are irrelevant in the context. We are here interested in conduct that brings about harm, whether it would ordinarily be said strictly to cause it or to contribute to, or occasion or facilitate it. Our concern is not with what are sometimes called "pure" omissions but with those that have harmful consequences. To eliminate causally irrelevant descriptions will drastically cut down the list of propositions describing conduct. For example, it may be clear that driving at 90 mph was a cause of the accident, but far from clear that not driving at 70 or 110 mph was. The propositions that the motorist did not drive at 70 or 110 mph leave open too many possibilities, some of which would not have brought about the harm that occurred but worse harm or none at all. Those propositions have to be rejected as not specific enough in the context.

12. For example, listing some of the things which the Prime Minister ought to have been doing instead of playing cricket.

The exact sort of harm in issue will influence the appropriate description in another way. A judge has said that a doctor's wrong diagnosis (a positive act) may be equivalent to his failure to make a proper diagnosis (an omission).[13] This suggests that in the context of responsibility for the consequences either description of the doctor's conduct is acceptable. That is not the case. Suppose a doctor diagnoses cancer rather than AIDS. If the harm to the patient comes about through his not getting the proper treatment for AIDS, the appropriate proposition about the doctor's conduct is that he did not diagnose AIDS. If, on the other hand, the patient suffers through being mistakenly treated for cancer, with bad side-effects, the relevant proposition is that the doctor mistakenly diagnosed cancer. The harm in these two cases is not the same.

The appropriate description of the conduct must be sensitive to the connection of the conduct with the exact harm for which the agent is said to be responsible. But when the harm is the same, the difference between doing and non-doing does not depend on the causal process by which the harm is brought about. There are negative as well as positive conditions of human welfare (absence of poison, availability of food) and the same is true, with the necessary adjustment, of keeping property in good condition. So harm can be done by either intrusion or deprivation: by introducing something noxious into the body or soil, or by removing or not supplying something necessary to its health. But whether harm comes about by intrusion or deprivation does not determine whether, if the causal process is traced further back, it will prove to have come about through doing or not-doing. Though often intrusions result from positive acts (beating, shooting, spraying, discharging effluent) and deprivations from not-doing-something (not feeding, not fertilizing) the inverse is possible. One can bring about starvation by destroying the food supply, a positive act. A doctor can allow a patient to be poisoned by a not-doing, for example, by not intervening when he knows that the nurse is about to give the patient a lethal dose by mistake.[14] In that case his not-doing results in an intrusion.

But what is it about the relevant description of conduct that makes it in substance positive or negative? It is widely thought, in my view

13. *Harnett* v. *Bond* [1924] 2 KB 517, 541.
14. Cf. Malm, *Killing*, above n.3, at p.253.

rightly, that the distinction between doing and not-doing is ultimately connected with bodily movements, and that doing involves bodily movements in a way in which not-doing does not. But the connection is not straightforward. Of the causally relevant descriptions of an agent's conduct on a given occasion, some may involve conscious bodily movement, others not ("the surgeon cut the artery" and "the surgeon did not see where the knife was going" are both relevant if the surgeon cut the artery because he did not see where the knife was going). Confronted with such ambiguities, how can we say whether the relevant proposition describing the conduct is positive or negative?

Though his detailed argument is rather complicated, a suggestion by Jonathan Bennett offers a useful hint in all but freakish cases. His suggestion is along the following lines. For an agent's conduct to be regarded as positive: (1) he must have moved in a way that was relevant to the outcome in the sense of causing it or raising the probability that it would occur, and (2) only that movement or a small number of closely related movements would have had the same outcome.[15] Thus, if the agent removes a rock from behind the wheel of a truck so that it slides downhill, his conduct can be described as positive because only that very movement or a small number of related movements by the agent would have ensured that the rock was removed so that the truck slid downhill. If, on the other hand, the agent refrains from putting the rock behind the wheel when he could do so, and the vehicle runs downhill in consequence, his conduct counts as negative. This is because there are many alternative bodily movements that the agent may have been performing (going for a walk, eating a sandwich, mending a leaking tap) such that, if he was doing them at the relevant time, he was not preventing the vehicle running downhill.[16] So it would not be wrong to say that the vehicle ran down hill because he was going for a walk or doing any one of a thousand other things. (The same would, of course, be true, if he was not doing anything, but it is not essential that he should have been doing nothing). It is the range of movements relevant to the outcome that determines whether his conduct is positive or negative. If there

15. Bennett, *Morality*, above n.4, at p.55f. Bennett confines his formulation to raising the probability of the harm. I have put it in what seems a more plausible form.
16. The examples come from Bennett, *Morality*, above n.4, at pp.52–3.

are a small number of related movements such that they would have ensured the outcome that came about, and the agent performed one of them, the conduct is positive, if a large number, it is negative.

The distinction suggested, though serviceable, is not infallible. Bizarre cases can be suggested, for example, those in which only immobility on the agent's part will bring about a harmful consequence.[17] Take a case in which John is searching for Dick to shoot him. The slightest movement on Bill's part will alert Dick to John's threat, in which case Dick will escape. If Bill remains immobile, and Dick is shot, was Bill's immobility a positive or negative instrumentality in Dick's death? On the suggested test it is negative, in that it does not involve movement, but positive in that there is no range of (alternative) movements that would have brought about the same outcome. In fact, any movement would have brought about a different outcome. It is worth noting, however, that fanciful cases do not make for sound judgement.[18] Our thought and language may mark out workable distinctions, even though on freakish hypotheses, they give indeterminate or counter-intuitive results. We should perhaps frankly concede that, on the suggested definition, Bill's conduct could be classed as either positive or negative.

The suggested distinction between positive and negative conduct, which depends on the way in which the agent's conscious bodily movements (or lack of them) are related to the outcome in which we are interested, is morally neutral. But it does in my view, at a deeper level, reflect a certain view of what it is to intervene in the world, and hence of responsibility. Why should bodily movement mark such a divide in our thought and language? Has the distinction a rationale?

A close study of causal language and thought suggested that the reason why movements feature so prominently in our assessment of responsibility is that we have a picture of the world as a matrix into which, by our movements and especially our manipulation of objects, we introduce changes.[19] By moving their bodies people change the world, though they may not know or foresee exactly what changes

17. Bennett, *Morality*, above n.4, at p.66; Malm, *Killing*, above n.3 at p.253 has an implausible example in which both immobility and activity (rowing) will cause harm, but to different people.
18. Bennett, *Morality*, above n.4, at p.74.
19. H.LA. Hart and T. Honoré, *Causation in the Law* [hereafter *Causation*] (2nd ed. Oxford 1985) pp.28–32.

will come about. It is inherent in this world-picture that positive acts count as interventions in the outside world and attract at least a minimal responsibility for their outcomes.[20] On the other hand, non-movement is prima facie not an intervention in the outside world, so that the agent is not responsible for its consequences. But superimposed on this picture of the world is a refinement of it, which treats disruptions of the normal course of events as similar to interventions that bring about change,[21] though the change is not now a change in the existing state of affairs but rather in the normal or expected sequence of events. The regular course of things may take the form not only of recurrent natural events, but of regular human conduct such as clearing the street when snow stops falling. If this regular or expected conduct fails to occur, the failure then counts not, as the first world-view would suggest, as a non-intervention but rather, on a wider view of what amounts to change, as a sort of intervention in the world. If, as is often (though not always) the case, the break in routine violates a norm (the person who does not sweep up the snow may or may not have a duty to do so), it is a form of not-doing that amounts to an omission and is a potential ground of responsibility.

I suggest, therefore, that what explains the difference between doing and not-doing is the notion of intervening in the world so as to bring about change; and that at a secondary level this notion extends to the interruption of human routines. If the human routine is required by a norm, the violation of it is an omission that will entail responsibility.

It was said at the beginning of this section that "omission" is a pejorative term. The point may now be spelled out. A not-doing that contributed to a favourable outcome, even if it has normative significance, does not count as an omission. If I refrain from vetoing a project that I have a right to veto, and the project is successful, my not vetoing it may be morally or legally significant, perhaps praiseworthy, but it is not an omission. If on the other hand I refrain from vetoing a disastrous project, which I had the right to veto, that might be an omission; but if it was, the reason would be that it was not merely my right but my duty to intervene. Not-doing when one has a duty to act

20. Above, pp.6, 10, 12.

21. Hart and Honoré, *Causation*, above n.19, at pp.33–8.

and not-doing when one has a right to act are not symmetrical notions.

3. Omissions and Distinct Duties

This section concentrates on distinct duties. It deals with the grounds on which distinct duties are imposed by legal systems and moral theories, and argues that, when a distinct duty is violated, acts and omissions are on a par, or very nearly so. Legal systems and moral theories do, of course, differ greatly in detail both among themselves and *vis-à-vis* one another as regards the circumstances in which they impose a distinct duty. My contention is not that they coincide, but that, if distinct duties are recognised at all, legal systems and moral theories agree on the broad grounds for imposing such duties to act. For example, they agree that the fact that someone is better placed than anyone else to help another is sometimes a ground for imposing a duty on him to help the other. But they may not agree on whether a motorist who, without fault, has run someone over has a duty to give aid to the victim.

I shall say no more about the optimizing theories (Section 2) since these do not recognise distinct as opposed to background duties. On the optimizing theories there is never a moral difference between acts and omissions where the outcome is the same. According to the optimizing theories, the agent has a general duty to intervene whenever to do so would optimize the chosen good. But these theories are oppressive, since instead of allowing an area of freedom where the agent can do as he likes within the limits of the largely negative background duties he owes to others, they require the overall optimum to be kept in sight every minute of the day. They make it impossible for people to pursue their own projects without continual distraction.

Those committed to law or to moral theories that embrace distinct duties argue differently. For them, an important class of omissions arise from distinct duties, which usually require both positive acts and abstentions. Distinct duties are limited and heterogeneous. The breach of such a duty to act will be a (distinct) omission, the breach of a duty to abstain a (distinct) commission. Alongside distinct duties there remain background duties to avoid doing harm and to help others in situations outside the limits set. But the background duties are weaker than the distinct duties, and the latter may themselves be of differing strengths.

Five types of situation that yield distinct duties can be listed.[22] Such a duty is often imposed on: (A) a person who performs a harmful or risk-creating act; (B) a person who occupies an office or position of responsibility or social role; (C) a person who is better placed than others to meet the need of someone dependent on him; (D) a person who has received a benefit from another; and (E) a person who has undertaken the duty in question. There is a good deal of overlap between these grounds of duty, and often more than one is present. In discussing these grounds I introduce a few examples from legal cases by way of illustration only. The grounds are as much moral as legal, assuming that the moral outlook adopted gives weight to duties. Only the extent of their application varies from society to society and, for practical reasons and out of respect for freedom, is usually broader in morals than in law.

A. Harmful and Risk-creating Acts

An important ground of duty is that the agent, by a positive act, has intervened or proposes to intervene in the world in such a way as to do harm, or create or substitute a new risk of harm, or increase an existing risk to others.[23] The agent then often has a duty to minimise the risk of harm, or, if it has occurred, to mitigate it by means that may be either positive or negative, usually both.

This duty is in principle distinct from any duty the agent may have violated in doing the harm or creating the risk of it in the first place. It is true that the two in practice often run together, so that creating the risk of harm and failing to take steps to avoid it are seen as part of a single course of wrongful conduct (for example, driving and not slowing down at the traffic lights). But that the duty to avoid threatened harm or minimise actual harm is secondary may be seen from the fact that the harm-doing or risk-creating act may not itself be culpable.[24] If I lend a car to a friend and later discover that the steering

22. There is a good discussion of duties in tort law in *Prosser and Keeton on Torts* (5th ed., St Paul, Minnesota, 1984) [hereafter *Torts*] para. 56. Cf. *Restatement of Torts* (*Second*) topic 7, "Duties of Affirmative Action", paras. 314–28.
23. Prosser and Keeton, *Torts*, at p.377.
24. *Restatement of Torts* (*Second*), para. 321.

is defective, I must warn the friend even though I did nothing wrong in lending the car. A motorist who without fault runs someone over has morally, and in many systems, legally, a duty to summon help,[25] even though he was not at fault in running the victim over.

Quite apart from these everyday instances, most economic and domestic activities, from building, manufacture, transport, and marketing to running a home, shop, school, or business create some risk to others. Those who engage in these activities are often required to take steps to minimise the risks involved, steps that vary from country to country and activity to activity, according to the level of wealth and social consciousness and the specific requirements of local law and custom.

This reaction to risk-creating acts and activities accounts for the legal doctrine that prior positive conduct can generate a duty to act. So to state the matter is misleading, because the positive act need not precede the time at which the precaution should have been taken. When the duty arises from doing harm, for example, running over a pedestrian, the positive act does precede the duty. But when the duty arises from creating a risk of harm, this need not be the case. True, a driver who takes a vehicle on the road must from then on keep a proper look-out, but he must not take the vehicle on the road in the first place unless it is roadworthy. He must ensure that it is roadworthy before taking it on the road. This duty is imposed not because of a previous act but because of a prospective, future act. Nothing turns on the sequence in time of risk-creating act and precautionary duty. The crucial factor is that the act, past or future, carries with it a danger to the person or property of others, and so may impose on the agent positive as well as negative duties.

This ground of duties to act is of the greatest conceptual and practical importance. Acts that do, or create risks of, harm are the prime example of noxious or potentially noxious human interventions in the world. Harmful omissions normally presuppose and are predicated on positive interventions, which they fail to counteract. Failure to react appropriately cannot be equated with doing harm or creating a risk of it in the first instance. This is an argument for the view that, in many contexts, positive acts are morally and socially worse than omissions.

25. *Restatement of Torts* (*Second*), para. 322.

The ground of duties imposed to counteract doing harm or creating risks presupposes a voluntary element. There must have been a conscious bodily movement on the agent's part, often with a deliberate plan behind it. But the agent need not have agreed to assume or even have known of the duties that his act or activity would impose on him. Society subjects him to them willy-nilly if he does the act or engages in the activity in question. It offers him a stark choice. He may not do A without also doing or having done B. He may not drive without keeping a proper look-out, invite visitors before taking steps to see that his property is safe, sell food without having checked that it is fresh, run a company without publishing annual accounts. Freedom in a social framework, which is the only freedom on offer, is limited and conditional.

B. Office or Position of Responsibility

A second ground is that the agent occupies a position or office or fills a role that may require him to act positively. Parents,[26] friends, employers,[27] managers, owners and possessors of property,[28] officials public and private have duties of this sort and are guilty of omission if they fail to discharge them. The legal liability of innkeepers, common carriers, and possessors of land falls under this heading.[29] In contrast with the previous risk-creating type of situation, the person who has a duty to act need not have created the danger himself. For instance, it seems reasonable that a landowner on whose premises a fire starts, but who did not start it himself, should take steps to put it out.[30] As with (A), there is a voluntary element in this ground of duty. The person in question has chosen to fill the office or position or take on the role, but, again, once he has done so, he is saddled with the duties attaching to the post whether he agreed to take them on or knew of them or not. The freedom to take on offices, roles and positions is, once again, limited and conditional.

26. Id., para. 316.
27. Id., para. 314B.
28. Id., para. 318.
29. Id., para. 314A.
30. *Commonwealth* v. *Cali* 247 Mass. 20, 141 NE 510 (1923); *Goldman* v. *Hargrave* [1967] 1 AC 645.

C. Dependency: Being Well Placed to Meet a Need

The second ground of duty shades into a third, where society imposes a duty to act positively because of a need which the agent is well placed, often better placed than anyone else, to fulfil. Dependency, permanent or temporary, then generates a duty of help and protection. The dependency may be due to the choice of the person concerned, who puts himself in a position where he is better placed than anyone else to fulfil a certain need, for example, by taking custody of someone so as to deprive him of normal opportunities for looking after himself or being looked after.[31] But the dependency need not have been chosen. Parents who have become so by mistake and not choice still have duties to their children. Temporary dependency is important when Samaritan type duties to rescue are in issue and is mainly a matter of chance. Very often the case for saying that there is a moral or legal duty to help someone in danger is that the person who could help is at hand and better placed to do so than anyone else. Whatever the extent of Samaritan type duties ought to be,[32] an important ground for imposing them at all is dependency.

Even if the person on whom the duty is imposed is not in the best position to meet it, but merely in as good a position as others, there can be a strong case for imposing a duty to act, if necessary by selection. An example is compulsory military service. In this context we are not free; social needs override our wishes.

D. Benefit Received

A fourth ground of duty that often includes a duty to act positively, and so may lead to responsibility for omission, is the receipt of a benefit. It is commonplace that the receipt of a gift or of hospitality imposes an obligation (not usually legal) on the recipient. The law of restitution is concerned with the duty of the recipient of money or property to restore benefits which there is not good reason for him to retain. The same ground helps explain why those who earn or receive

31. *Restatement of Torts* (*Second*), para. 314A.
32. See T. Honoré, *Making Law Bind* (Oxford, 1987) ch.13.

money or enjoy facilities within a social framework are subject to tax liability. Progressive taxation illustrates ground (C), by which those who are better placed to meet collective needs are subject to a greater burden. This ground of duty often embraces a voluntary element, in that the person concerned has a choice whether to receive the benefit. Once he has done so he cannot escape from the resultant duty. His freedom is once more conditional. This type of duty does not always presuppose any positive conduct on the part of the person subject to it. A person who passively receives a benefit may be bound as a result.

E. Undertaking

There is no sharp divide between undertaking an office or receiving a benefit that carries duties with it and undertaking duties directly. But promising in particular gives the person undertaking the duty greater freedom to fix its content than in (A), (B) and (D). Promising depends on the invention of forms of words for binding oneself, and such an invention is possible only within a social context in which people understand definite duties which stem, as it were, naturally from the structure of a community, as they do in (A) to (D) above.

Promising is not the only form of voluntary undertaking. There can be conventions to the effect that non-verbal conduct carries with it a duty, and there is no very clear line between non-verbal undertakings on the one hand and taking on a role or receiving a benefit that involves duties on the other. One who in a supermarket puts goods on the check-out counter is taken to agree to pay for them. One who boards a bus must pay the fare to his destination. Is this because boarding a bus conventionally carries this meaning, or because the passenger has the benefit of the ride, or because he assumes the role of passenger? The categories overlap, and non-verbal conventions are often unclear in their implications. A good example, important in practice, is that of a householder who allows someone, family, friend or stranger, into his home for a cup of tea, as a guest at a party,[33] or for a shorter or longer visit. Opening the door and inviting in is significant, but what duty does it import if the visitor wants to stay on, or falls ill, or is reluctant to leave because of the weather,

33. *Parrish* v. *Truman* 124 Ariz. 228, 603 Pac. 2d 120, 121 (1979) says no duty to protect the guest against assault by three men who were allowed in and started a fight.

or has no alternative accommodation? Whatever undertaking is involved in inviting a person in may in the end merge into dependency as in (C) above.[34]

The grounds set out for imposing distinct duties, including positive duties, the violation of which amounts to an omission, do not fall into any neat pattern. The needs of the community (office-holding, risk-creation, dependency), justice between its members (benefit, dependency), and respect for choice of those who freely agree to take burdens on themselves (undertaking, risk-creation, office-holding), all help to explain one or more grounds. They seem not to derive from or be reducible to a single principle. It is worth noting that the three grounds of contractual liability, benefit, reliance, and expectation, are all represented: benefit under (D), reliance (causing loss by inducing expense) under (A), and expected gain under (E). There is no particular reason to suppose that the strength of the duties arising under these three heads need be the same.

4. Relative Culpability

It is time to return to the question whether an omission, other things being equal, is less culpable than a positive act that brings about the same or a similar outcome. On the optimizing or overall duty view of morality, acts and omissions always stand on a level. All depends on whether in the given situation the optimizing course is to act or to abstain from action. In settling this question costs have to be taken into account. They will often tilt the balance in favour of not-doing as less culpable, not in principle but in the particular case.

This optimizing view is counter-intuitive. It leaves unexplained why, as mentioned earlier (Section 1), acts and omissions are seldom equal in the resentment they cause. By and large, positive acts cause more resentment than omissions with similar results, though resentment is also affected by what is seen as the motive of the agent. I feel worse about Mark if he hits me than if he does not intervene, as he easily could have, to stop James hitting me (Mark is much stronger than James). The difference is not simply accounted for by the effort and danger involved in intervening in a fight. Here resentment has

34. *R* v. *Nicholls* 13 Cox 75 (1874).

partly to do with the feeling that Mark's blow points to a worse vice than his standing aside: ill will rather than lethargy or cowardice. But this may be because our assessment of vices reflects the distinction between positive acts and omissions. At any rate, feeling is in practice more often directed against the person who did the harm than the person who abstained from preventing it. Even when the harm is equal (despite the disparity of strength, Mark and James hit equally hard on this occasion) the agent is not regarded as on a level with the non-intervener. The reaction is more nearly equal when the abstainer is felt to have a distinct duty to intervene. If Mark is a friend of mine he ought to have protected me from James, but even so it was a worse provocation on his part actually to hit me. Indeed, I shall then resent Mark's blow more than James's. Though the blows are equal in the sense of equally painful, the blow from a friend is more insulting. Harm is here agent-relative. Mark makes my position worse, not just physically but from the point of view of friendship, whereas James does this only physically; and, as stressed earlier (Section 1), worsening one's position is more greatly resented than not making it better. It is an inroad on security, as opposed to an inroad on expectation.

On the distinct duties theory my resentment of Mark' blow is justified, because that theory recognises the distinct duties attaching to friendship. On that view omissions are sometimes morally the same or nearly the same as acts that bring about similar harm; but in other cases they are less culpable. They may be equally culpable when a person, by virtue of his office or role, has a distinct duty to a defined person or persons. Take the case of Susan, a nurse whose duty is to give a patient a certain medicine at six o'clock. Without a valid excuse she gives the wrong medicine or fails to give any medicine at all. Can her legal or moral culpability be different in the two cases, assuming that the impact on the patient's health is equally bad and that her character does not appear in a worse light in one of them (because, for example, in the second case she went off to watch a TV programme)? Her duty is to use the means, positive or negative, which will enable the patient to be restored to health. The same will be true if for some reason no nurse is available and Adrian, a chemist who knows what he is doing, undertakes to give the patient the proper medicine. It is equally bad of him to give the wrong medicine and to fail to give any medicine, again assuming the harm to the patient and the motivation to be similar. Suppose again that Adrian does not promise to give the medicine, but that he is the only person available to do so in an emergency. The act and omission will again be morally on a par. As this example shows, when a distinct duty exists, the fact that positive acts make greater demands on the person concerned than abstentions does not support the view, as it otherwise would, that an omission is less culpable that a positively harmful act. The argument from distinct duty counteracts the argument from cost.

Judgement is, however, clouded by the fact that it is very difficult to think of instances when the outcome of the acts and omissions are the same or closely similar. In the medicine example it is hardly plausible that giving the wrong medicine will have the same impact on the patient as failing to give any medicine at all. This difficulty has led to the devising of bizarre examples like that of the runaway trolley, of which more in a moment, in which an act and an omission do have very similar outcomes. One reason why it is not easy to think of examples in which the outcomes are the same is that an omission can more often be more easily parried than a positive act. If A gives B the wrong medicine, his intervention may be irremediable. There may be no antidote. If A does not give B the right medicine someone else may do so, or he may do it himself later. So the equivalence holds, at most, when no one but A is in a position to intervene, and that is precisely the sort of case on which, in the distinct duty theory, A may well have a duty to intervene.

There is, therefore, much to be said for considering a banal example in which an act and an omission have the same effect, and it would cost the same or much the same to avoid either. Take the problem of litter in the streets. If a person is employed by the local council to keep the streets clean, it can make no noticeable difference to the appearance of the street whether he drops a wrapper in the street himself or fails to pick up a wrapper dropped by someone else. The outcome in each case is that there is one more wrapper in the street than there would otherwise have been, and the urban scene is to that extent less tidy. It is nevertheless probably worse for him to drop a wrapper than to fail to pick one up, since he is in that way adding to the very conditions he is employed to remedy.

The difference is more obvious if we consider an ordinary pedestrian, who either drops a wrapper or fails to pick one up that he or someone else has dropped. Here dropping the wrapper is surely morally and socially worse. The litter problem exists only because people drop wrappers and other rubbish in the street and so disfigure the scene and, if the things are greasy, create a risk of slipping. Wrapper-dropping is antisocial in a way in which not picking up wrappers is not, because if nobody dropped wrappers the nuisance would not exist, whereas if everyone picked them up, or there was an efficient cleansing service, the nuisance would still exist until the wrappers were picked up. Conversely, for an ordinary pedestrian to pick up a wrapper is better than not dropping one, since to pick one up is to do more than one's duty, whereas it is no more than one's duty (a background duty) not to drop wrappers in the street.

This example is a good illustration of the greater moral blame attaching to positive acts, because the trouble involved in disposing of a wrapper neatly in bin or bag is much the same as the trouble involved in picking a wrapper up. The cost of not dropping the wrapper is therefore close to that of picking one up. The positive act of dropping the wrapper is worse, not because its outcome is more harmful or the alternative more costly, but because of the sort of harm- or risk-creating act it is.[35] It is an intervention that changes things for the worse. Only if one looks at items of conduct atomistically rather than in their wider setting – a fault of some lawyers and moral philosophers – do acts and omissions appear equivalent.

The litter problem is a paradigm. It is primarily by positive acts that people do harm and create risks of harm to others, in the sense of changing things for the worse, whether by violence, pollution, speed of movement, destruction of property, or in a score of other ways. Of course, this view of the primary threats to our individual and collective well-being depends on our living in a relatively stable (as it were, Newtonian) world, in which people and objects on the whole continue as they are unless something intervenes to change them. People reasonably attach importance to this continuity since their survival and that of others depends on it. This aim of survival in a stable state and the flourishing of which it is a condition is one that people can generally ensure, provided that others do not intrude on them or destroy what they need. Security in this sense is therefore a prime human value, and any conduct that threatens to change it for the worse a prime evil.

35. Conversely, positive acts which constitute achievements and improve the world are socially and morally better than abstentions from obstructing the achievements.

This helps to explain, I believe, why positive harm-doing is on the whole viewed as worse than harmful abstention, which threatens our security interests only indirectly. Though in a particular instance a harmful abstention may have equally noxious results, in general, positive acts of intrusion and destruction are the more menacing, and it is reasonable to judge them more severely from a social and moral point of view. To say this is not to recommend a form of rule-utilitarianism, though it is certainly a sound principle of conduct to abstain from harmful intrusions and acts of destruction. It is rather that harmful positive acts have a general destructive significance different from that of harmful abstentions.

The great value placed on security explains why making someone's position worse is for good reason seen as worse that not making it better. The latter threatens not security so much as the expectation of improvement, which is a different but secondary value, because it presupposes stability. Atiyah is therefore, in my view, right to argue that in contract law expectation damage is less significant, and calls less urgently for compensation, than loss through reliance.

The value attaching to stability also helps to explain when omissions and abstentions are seen as threatening, which they clearly sometimes are, for otherwise disruptive strikes would not be feared. They are so judged when security has come to depend on homeostatic routines, and when disruptions of security by harmful and risk-creating acts are remedied by similar routines, which then fail.

Viewed against this background in which security is the prime value, worsening interventions – acts that make things worse or create a risk that they will be worse – must generally be more objectionable than failures to intervene. The latter are for the most part secondary in one of two ways. Either they fail to make things better rather than making them worse, and so violate our secondary rather than our primary interests; or they constitute failures to react against worsening interventions. Their secondary character seems to justify the judgement that harmful abstentions are normally less culpable than positive acts, even though in the context of distinct duties, as we have seen, the two are usually on a level.

In conclusion, it may be worth turning briefly to one of the dramatic examples that have been invented to test the relative culpability of positive acts and omissions. These are examples where intuitive judgement is to be mistrusted. If the examples are very gruesome they numb our sensibilities,[36] and if very remote from everyday life outstrip our moral resources. Suppose the agent has a choice between A's death and B's. A trolley-car[37] is out of control and will crush Tom unless I pull a lever, in which case the trolley will crush Sam. If we know no more than this – there is no information about my role and how I come to be in a position to intervene – the right conclusion is that I should not intervene. The act of pulling the lever and crushing Sam would be worse than letting the trolley take its course. As Malm points out, I could in no way justify my intervention to Sam's family and friends.[38] On the other hand I can justify my non-intervention to Tom's family, because I had no authority and no business to intervene. This judgement of course presupposes that harmful interventions have to be justified, even if I am redirecting the harm rather than increasing it.

The reason against pulling the lever is not happily expressed by saying that I should not play God. There are many less exalted roles that would justify intervention. If I am an official of the trolley company in charge of the lever mechanism, I may well have a reason connected with the overall effect on the system to pull the lever. In that case, the consequences of intervention and non-intervention are not the same, and this difference will have to be taken into account in reaching a decision. Again, if an army commander diverts the enemy fire from point A to point B, where an equal number of casualties is to be expected, he may be justified in doing so because of the tactical advantage to be gained. Indeed he may be justified even if heavier casualties are likely. Here again the outcome is not the same.

To revert to the trolley-car, if the person who pulled the lever was Tom's father, this would at least make his intervention less culpable than if he were a stranger to both Tom and Sam, for the outcome to him if Tom dies is then different from that if Sam dies. But these examples point to the importance in making the comparison between acts and omissions of two factors. One is the social role of the agent, which may carry with it a distinct duty that adds to the reasons in favour of intervention. The other is that, in the trolley-car type of case, intervening by a positive act is worse than not intervening,

---

36. R. Trammell in *Killing and Letting Die* (ed. B. Steinbock, 1980) p.167.
37. J.J. Thompson, "The Trolley Problem", in *Essays on Moral Theory* (Harvard, 1986) pp.94–116.
38. Malm, *Killing*, above n.3, at pp.245–8.

unless the outcome of not intervening is worse than that of intervening for some reason other than that one person dies. When outcomes are equal, abstention is the appropriate course for those who lack the right or duty to intervene. It would be strange to think otherwise.

4

THE MORALITY OF TORT LAW: QUESTIONS AND ANSWERS[1]

> In relation to any social institution, after stating what general aim or value its maintenance fosters, we should inquire whether there are any, and if so what, principles limiting the unqualified pursuit of this aim or value.[2]
>
> H.L.A. Hart

1. The Questions Posed

Hart was writing about punishment. In his view, those who are puzzled about the justification of punishment should begin by disentangling a number of questions about the criminal process. It is a mistake to search for a single justification (deterrence or retribution) for the system as a whole. Moreover, once we see that a single aim will not justify every aspect of the system, we should not replace the single aim by a compound aim. We should not, for example, say that the justification of punishment is a mixture of deterrence, retribution, reform and denunciation. At least six questions about punishment need to be answered separately: (1) Why are certain kinds of conduct forbidden by law on pain of punishment? (2) What is the definition of punishment? (3) What general aims justify us in having a system of criminal law? (4) Who may properly be punished? (5) Subject to what mental and other conditions may a person be punished? and (6) How much punishment are we justified in inflicting? The answers to questions (4) to (6), which concern the "distribution" of punishment,

1. First published in *Philosophical Foundations of Tort Law* (ed. David G.Owen, Oxford, 1995) pp.73–95.
2. H.L.A. Hart, *Punishment and Responsibility. Essays in the Philosophy of Law* 10 (Oxford, 1968) [hereafter *Punishment and Responsibility*].

limit the extent to which it is proper to pursue the general aims that emerge in answer to (3).

Hart's remark was meant to apply to institutions other than criminal law, and it can certainly be applied to tort law. The theory of tort law is now the subject of a sophisticated debate, especially in North America.[3] But has enough groundwork been done in distinguishing the various questions to be answered? This essay tries to unravel some of the questions and to suggest some answers.

Tort law and criminal law have common features. Each aims to eliminate or reduce undesirable behaviour, each provides for sanctions to be imposed on those whose conduct is undesirable, and each poses difficult questions about the conditions for imposing sanctions and the extent of liability of wrongdoers. On the other hand the aims of the tort system are in some ways wider than those of the criminal justice system; and, corresponding to this, the definition of tort liability differs from that of punishment.

Here are some questions about tort law corresponding to those put by Hart about criminal law. We may ask (1) Why are certain types of conduct made tortious? (2) What is the definition of tort liability? (3) What general aims justify the state in maintaining a system of tort law? (4) What justifies the person whose rights have been infringed in claiming compensation from the wrongdoer? (5) Subject to what conditions may one who by his conduct has infringed the rights of another be required to pay compensation? and (6) What limits should be placed on the amount of compensation payable?

Only the moral aspect of these questions will be examined. Efficiency, and its elaboration by Richard Posner,[4] are left on one side, as are problems of proof. Tort law, like the rest of law, must satisfy several values, of which efficiency in pursuing worthwhile objectives is only one.[5] Efficiency must be pursued within a morally

3. See Richard W. Wright, "Substantive Corrective Justice", 77 *Iowa Law Rev.* 625 (1992) (discussing the work of Jules L.Coleman and Ernest J.Weinrib). See generally Symposium, "Corrective Justice and Formalism – The Care One Owes One's Neighbours", 77 *Iowa Law Rev.* 403 (1992).

4. See e.g. Richard Posner, "What has Pragmatism to Offer Law?", 63 *S.Cal. Law Rev.* 1653, 1657, 1662–3 (1990).

5. "Tort law implements a variety of different principles and policies": Jules L. Coleman, "The Mixed Conception of Corrective Justice", 77 *Iowa Law Rev.* 427, 427 (1992) [hereafter *Mixed Conception*]; cf. Jules L. Coleman, "Tort Law and the Demands of Corrective Justice", 67 *Ind. Law J.* 349, 357 (1992) [hereafter *Tort Law and Demands*].

defensible framework;[6] so we must ask, and ask first, what aims it is morally defensible to pursue by imposing tort liability.

2. The Questions Answered

A. The Descriptive Framework of Tort Law

The first two questions listed, though concerned with norms, call for descriptive, not normative answers.

1. Why are certain types of conduct made tortious?

The first question Hart asked in his analysis of criminal law was why certain kinds of conduct are forbidden by law and so made crimes or offences. He gave the answer "to announce to society that these actions are not to be done and to secure that fewer of them are done".[7] The same may be said of the conduct that by common law or statute is made a tort. When the legislature or courts make conduct a tort they mean, by stamping it as wrongful, to forbid or discourage it or, at a minimum, to warn those who indulge in it of the liability they may incur. It is true that the terms used to describe it, "tortious" or "wrongful", are not as strong as the term "offence" in criminal law, and do not carry the same stigma. But that is a matter of degree. In tort law not only actions but omissions are at times treated as wrongful; that is also the case in criminal law, for example in the law of homicide. Again, tort law sometimes treats as wrongful not an action or omission as such but the causing of harm by conduct of a potentially dangerous sort, for example selling a defective product or setting off explosives. In such cases the harm-causing action itself need not be wrongful, though it is done at the agent's risk. Criminal law also uses this technique, mostly with the implication that the conduct is wrongful even apart from its consequences. Think

6. Ernest J. Weinrib, "The Case for a Duty to Rescue", 90 *Yale Law J.* 247, 263 (1980); Guido Calabresi, *The Cost of Accidents: A Legal and Economic Analysis* (1970) pp.24–6, 291–308. For a view that this leaves minimal room for the pursuit of efficiency, see Richard W. Wright, "The Efficiency Theory of Causation and Responsibility: Unscientific Formalism and False Semantics", 63 *Chi.-Kent Law Rev.* 552, 562–7 (1987).
7. Hart, above n.2, p.6.

of the crime (in the UK) of causing death by dangerous driving, dangerous driving being itself an offence, though a less serious one. The word that best covers all these cases (actions, omissions, causing untoward consequences) is "conduct". If conduct is understood to include them all, we can say that tort law, like criminal law, announces that certain conduct is forbidden and tries to secure that less of it takes place. Tortious conduct is generally wrongful in itself, though if no harm results no liability may be incurred. When strict liability is imposed the conduct is generally not wrongful in itself, but the wrong consists in causing harm by engaging in risky activities.

But that is not the only reason why the state and its courts make conduct tortious. One point of creating a tort, as opposed to a crime, is to define and give content to people's rights by providing them with a mechanism for protecting them and securing compensation if their rights are infringed.

2. What is the definition of tort liability?

The second question follows naturally from the first. It concerns the definition of tort liability. Liability in tort is imposed, (a) if the dispute cannot be resolved without litigation, by the courts of the legal system having jurisdiction (b) at the instance of an individual whose right has been infringed (c) on a person who has committed a civil wrong (tort) against that person and (d) normally imposes on one who has committed the wrong an obligation to pay money by way of compensation to the person whose right has been infringed.[8] One may treat as subsidiary, though theoretically important, other remedies in tort law such as mandatory orders or injunctions and, outside tort law, administrative measures that may impose pecuniary penalties for such conduct.

B. The Justifying Aims of Tort Law

The first two questions called for a description of how the system of tort law operates. The answers did not serve to justify the existence of tort law, still less any particular part of it. The third question concerns the justification of tort law:

8. See Wright, above n.3, at p.634 n.38.

3. What general aims justify the state in maintaining a system of tort law?

Two different aspects of this question need to be dealt with here: (a) is the state entitled to take steps to discourage undesirable behaviour? and (b) if so, may it do so by treating certain interests of individuals as rights and giving them the legal power to protect those rights and obtain compensation if they are violated?

The tort system is one means by which the state, on behalf of the community, seeks to reduce conduct that it sees as undesirable. Others include the criminal law, education, administrative means such as licensing and inspection, differential taxes and many more. The state not only may but must, if a society is to be viable, try to minimize at least some types of disruptive conduct. Is tort law, like criminal law, a suitable means to this end? What tort and criminal law have in common, and what distinguishes them from some other means of social control, is that they work by marking out conduct, or the failure to attain a required standard of conduct, as wrongful. On the other hand licensing, inspection, differential taxation and rationing discourage behaviour, not by marking it as wrongful but by limiting opportunities to indulge in it, for example by refusing licences for sex shops; or by denying benefits to those who do indulge in it, for example by charging more for leaded petrol. Other branches of the law of civil responsibility, such as the law of contracts or restitution, though they provide remedies for what are seen as wrongs, act primarily not by treating conduct as wrongful but in other ways. Contract law mainly marks out the conditions in which agreements will be enforceable and the law of restitution mainly specifies what is to count as an unjust benefit.

The technique of tort law is therefore to label certain things as not to be done or omitted or brought about, though in a less stigmatic way than criminal law. If the state is justified in making conduct criminal and attaching to it penalties that may include prison, it must also be justified in marking conduct as tortious and attaching to it the lesser sanction of compensation. In all societies some people behave disruptively or, without meaning to be disruptive, expose others to undue risks of injury. The state must have the right and duty to minimize the risks and remedy the disruption.

But it does not follow that the legislature or courts are right to make any particular sort of conduct tortious. That must depend on factors like those familiar in the debate about criminal law. Is the state justified in rendering tortious (or criminal) only conduct that threatens harm to others? If so, must the harm be physical/economic, or should inroads on personal, emotional and immaterial interests count as harm? This is not the place to pursue this important debate.

Assuming that the state can rightly make conduct tortious, is it entitled to do so by treating individual interests as rights and threatening economic sanctions against those who infringe the rights? Can the state properly use its resources, prestige and power for this purpose? The question goes deep into political theory. A supporter of the rule of law, and hence of the *Rechtstaat*[9] idea, is driven to a positive answer. The rule of law depends, among other factors, on a framework of individual rights that must be respected by others and by the state itself. This gives people a degree of independence from one another and from the power of government. One who accepts this ideal will think the state justified in trying to minimize undesirable behaviour by a technique that treats some interests as rights and gives those who have the rights the power to avert or redress the unwanted conduct.

Assuming that this is a proper role for the state, it may also be justified, within limits, in subsidizing right-holders by setting up and paying for a framework of civil courts for the enforcement of tort claims. But even a critic who is not in principle opposed to the rule of law can argue that to subsidize private rights in this way is not a proper use of the state's resources. While, so far as I know, there is no state in which this view has so far been taken, it may be rash in an age of privatization to assume that none will in future refuse to subsidize the use of its courts to give effect to the tort system. In such a state, those who pursue tort claims in the courts would have to pay the cost of judicial enforcement. It would be morally and politically objectionable for a state to go even further and refuse access to its courts to those wishing to bring claims in tort. Closing the courts to tort claims would be to give up an important technique for lessening undesirable conduct, and would jettison a central element in the structure of rights that underlies the rule of law. Of course in some societies (past and present), more emphasis is placed on reducing bad conduct by

9. The idea that the state has a duty to set out and enforce certain rights of the citizen, even against itself.

social pressures and administrative means than by the enforcing individual rights. But these societies tend to be less committed to the rule of law.

Assuming that the arguments in favour of the rule of law are persuasive, the state is justified in maintaining a system of tort law that seeks to reduce the incidence of undesirable conduct by treating certain interests of individuals as rights and providing those who have them with the legal power to avert inroads on those rights and, if they are infringed, to obtain compensation for their violation.

C. The Distribution of Tort Liability

4. What justifies the person whose rights have been infringed in claiming compensation from the wrongdoer?

What was said in answer to question (3) is incomplete. To justify the tort system, it is not enough to show that the state is entitled to take steps to minimize undesirable behaviour and to give individuals the power to protect their rights and obtain compensation if they are violated. It must also be shown that some principle or principles of justice entitle the right-holders (tort-plaintiffs) to sue the wrongdoers (tort-defendants) for compensation. For though the state may be entitled to designate certain interests as rights and certain sorts of conduct as wrongs, it cannot thereby make it *just* for the right-holders to sue the wrongdoers for compensation. It cannot by fiat create a principle of justice linking the two. The issue here is then whether there are one or more independent principles that justify tort claims against tort-defendants.

a. Corrective Justice

The principle most often cited is that of corrective justice.[10] This can be put in various ways. On a wide view it requires those who have without justification harmed others by their conduct to put the matter right.[11] This they must do on the basis that harm-doer and harm-sufferer are to be treated as equals, neither more deserving than the

10. Wright, above n.3, pp.627–31.
11. The application of corrective justice to unjust gains is not dealt with here, though a similar analysis would be possible.

other. The one is therefore not entitled to become relatively better off by harming the other. The balance must be restored.

I have said "without justification" rather than "wrongfully", not because the latter is incorrect, but to put aside the question whether to harm someone without justification is a wrong in itself[12] or whether it is a wrong only if the person doing the harm was at fault. "Putting the matter right" (reparation)[13] is a concept that may, according to the circumstances, require the harm-doer to restore something to the person harmed, or to repair a damaged object or (when the unharmed position cannot be restored, as it usually cannot) to compensate the harm-sufferer. Compensating in turn means doing something conventionally regarded as restoring the harm-sufferer to his unharmed position. "Compensate" is used to cover whatever may be done to make good the loss when reparation is not literally possible; what counts as compensation is largely a matter of convention. Nothing in the idea of corrective justice requires the compensation to be in money. Though in tort law it nearly always takes that form, outside of tort law various forms of substitute provision in kind or services are treated as proper ways of making good the harm to the sufferer.[14]

The claim to put things right lies against the harm-doer, and sometimes only the harm-doer can satisfy it, for example because what is called for includes an apology. But in other cases, for instance when the claim is purely for money, the harm-doer can arrange for someone else to pay, perhaps through third-party insurance or the generosity of a friend. If the matter is put right in that way, the

12. On the wrong-in-itself view, which I prefer, the defendant's conduct may not be *wrongful in itself*, but causing harm without justification is nevertheless a *wrong* that grounds a claim for compensation. Jules Coleman expresses it differently: "the duty to repair . . . wrongful losses is grounded not in the fact that they are the result of wrongdoing, but in the fact that the losses are the injurer's responsibility, the result of the injurer's agency". Coleman, *Mixed Conception*, above n.5, at p.443. Unlike Coleman, I regard the two as correlative: the losses are wrongful if and only if caused by the agent without justification.

13. Neil MacCormick, *Legal Right and Social Democracy* (1982) p.212.

14. Contrary to Coleman, *Tort Law and Demands*, above n.5, at p.366, Wright argues that in cases where corrective justice requires the rightful position to be restored, the mode of rectification is implicit in the grounds of recovery and liability: see Wright, above n.3, at p.683. But, unless settled by a particular legal system, the precise content of the victim's right and the appropriate mode of giving effect to it against the harm-doer seems an open question, though the rectification must be adequate in context.

harm-doer satisfies the demands of corrective justice.[15] Moreover, the loss may be covered by the harm-sufferer's own insurance, or through a state scheme, in which case the harm-doer may to that extent be freed from the need to compensate the harm-sufferer. The harm-doer has wrongfully caused the physical harm but, ultimately, not an economic loss. But then the harm-doer, not having satisfied the liability personally, may not unjustly be required to compensate the insurer or the state instead of compensating the harm-sufferer. In law this takes the form of subrogation.

From what has been said it will be clear that in my view corrective justice is a relational principle. It can exist only when the harm-doer's wrong violates the harm-sufferer's right; the two cannot be dissociated. On this point I agree with Weinrib and disagree with the view formerly embraced by Jules Coleman. For Coleman at one time thought that there could be wrongful losses, calling for redress, in the abstract, even though one could not point to any particular wrongdoer as the person who ought to put them right.[16]

Corrective justice presupposes that the defendant has caused harm to the plaintiff. It is this doing of harm that needs to be corrected. So there must be a causal link between the defendant's conduct and the plaintiff's loss. The conduct need not be *the* cause of the harm.[17] It is enough that it is *a* cause, and there can be more than one human cause of the harm in question, in which case both (or all) harm-doers can be responsible.[18] The existence of the causal link is a *necessary* condition of corrective justice and of the duty to compensate in a tort action. It is not a *sufficient* condition, however, for two reasons. First, for compensation to be rightly claimed, there must have been no justification for inflicting the harm. If there was a justification, the person harmed cannot on the same facts be justified in claiming compensation. Secondly, though someone who harms another without justification must in principle make the harm good as a matter of corrective justice, what form his responsibility should take, whether legal or extra-legal, and subject to what further conditions,[19] remains an open question.

15. Wright, *Corrective Justice*, above n.3, at p.703.
16. Not entirely abandoned in his *Mixed Conception*, above n.5.
17. Stephen R. Perry, "The Moral Foundations of Tort Law", 77 *Iowa Law Rev.* 449, 464, n.58 (1992) [hereafter *Moral Foundations*].
18. See below, question (6).
19. See below, question (6).

Since a causal link is necessary to both corrective justice and tort liability, much turns on the view we take of the responsibility of one who causes another harm. A widespread view is that a person who harms another is responsible for the harm only when he is at fault.[20] If this view is accepted, corrective justice has to be defined more narrowly than in my earlier formulation. It will require reparation or compensation only if the person causing the harm was at fault in doing so. This view would set a narrower limit to corrective justice and, in particular, would exclude strict liability in tort law.[21] On the wider view, which I favour, the importance of fault is not denied, but the fault requirement operates, so far as it does, as an independent limit to the pursuit of corrective justice rather than as an element in it. If so, it falls to be discussed under the next question (5), which concerns the conditions for imposing tort liability.

b. Outcome Responsibility

The view that those who cause harm are responsible for it even in the absence of fault fits what I have elsewhere termed outcome responsibility.[22] On this view we are, if of full capacity and hence in a position to control our behaviour, responsible for the outcome of our conduct, whether act or omission.[23] This responsibility is an essential constituent of our character and identity, without which we would lack both achievements and failures. Lacking a positive history of what we had done and its outcome), we should at most be half-persons.[24] Outcome responsibility figures prominently in our sense

---

20. E.g. Coleman, *Mixed Conception*, above n.5, 442–443; Perry, above n.17, at p.497.
21. I take strict liability to be liability without fault, whether or not the defendant was engaged in a dangerous activity. To engage in a dangerous activity gives the law a reason to impose strict liability on the person engaging in it, but does not form part of the definition of strict liability. Wright, interpreting Aristotle, takes a different view, distinguishing between strict liability for risk and absolute liability: Wright, above n.3, at p.697 n.335. But are Aristotle's "unjust losses" not simply those caused by another without justification, for example by accident, even if the conduct did not apparently carry with it any special risk?
22. Above pp.27, 31–2.
23. Cf. Perry, above n.17, pp.488–9. My thesis can stand on its own feet. But it is arguable that Aristotle took a similar view viz. that wrongful, mistaken and accidental conduct (covering both fault and strict liability) causing harm to others obliges the harm-doer to repair the harm as a matter of corrective justice. Wright, above n.3, at pp.697–8.
24. The other "negative" half of our history concerns what has happened to us.

of our own agency and is important for both the theory of agency and moral theory.[25] This is not to say that we are responsible for everything that would not have happened had we not acted, or refrained from acting, as we did.[26] That would be a misconception. The conduct that grounds outcome responsibility includes what we do, but does not include our not doing all that we do not do. Under non-doing it comprises only omissions, and an omission is the violation of a norm.[27]

There is nothing mysterious about this limitation of our responsibility to actions and those omissions that violate norms. When we act we launch ourselves upon the world and implicitly choose to be responsible for what we do, including its outcome. When we do *not* act we are responsible only so far as responsibility is thrust upon us, because society requires of us certain actions that we omit to do. Moreover, the outcomes to which outcome responsibility applies do not consist of everything that would not have happened but for the conduct in question, but are limited to consequences properly attributable to the conduct rather than to later voluntary or abnormal interventions by other people and events.

Outcome responsibility serves to foster a sense of identity because it does not stretch indefinitely into the future but enables each of us to claim for ourselves, or to share with a few others, outcomes of limited extent, whether successes or failures.[28] Yet outcome responsibility for harm to another does not by itself create a duty to compensate.

25. Perry, *Moral Foundations*, above n.17, at p.490.
26. As argued by Wright, above n.3, at p.682.
27. Above pp.46–54.
28. The discussion of outcome-responsibility here fits an analysis of causal concepts by Hart and myself that need not be repeated in this essay: see generally H.L.A. Hart and Tony Honoré, *Causation in the Law* (2nd ed. 1985), 68–83 [hereafter Hart and Honoré]. Stephen Perry treats this as an analysis of responsibility rather than causation: see Perry, above n.17, at p.503. But since our approach is regularly criticized for containing normative elements that are foreign to causation, it is worth stressing that the analysis of causal concepts that we put forward, though not normative, is functional. These causal concepts take the shape they do because they are tailored (of course not consciously) to fit certain purposes, especially explanation and the attribution of responsibility. Those purposes require them to incorporate cut-off points. Without cut-off points, both backward and forward, causal concepts would not play the prominent role they do in everyday life, because they would not serve any worthwhile purpose. But these concepts are not normative: they are neutral between different ways of behaving and different assessments of conduct. Thus, the responsibility that they serve to identify is as much responsibility for good conduct and good outcomes as for bad conduct and bad outcomes.

The form that our responsibility for an outcome should take remains an open question. An apology or telephone call will often be enough. But outcome responsibility is a basis on which the law can erect a duty to compensate if there is reason to do so. There will be some reason to do so if the conduct in question is socially undesirable and if there is also reason to treat the harm suffered as the infringement of a right.

If the outcome of conduct is harmful to another, the next question is whether in the context there was a *justification* for inflicting the harm. We are sometimes justified in injuring others, for example in self-defence. When we compete we are justified in inflicting losses or setbacks on our rivals. Whether those injuries, losses or setbacks count as "harm" depends on whether that protean word is thought to carry with it the implication that the injury or loss has not been justifiably inflicted.[29] I win the one hundred metres and you lose. Outcome responsibility makes me responsible for your defeat as well as for my victory. But the nature of the race justifies me in inflicting that setback on you. The same is true of other forms of competition, for example in trade, business, politics, literature, and love. If some succeed, others fail. When, however, there is no justification for inflicting a loss on another, outcome-responsibility supports the claims of corrective justice. Since I am responsible for a loss inflicted on you without justification, I have a duty to answer for what I have done, and to make whatever amends are appropriate to the situation. It will then be in order for the state to impose tort liability to compel me to make good your loss, if my conduct was undesirable and your loss an infringement of your rights, provided that to do so is not inconsistent with other values important to maintain.[30]

c. Distributive Justice

But if outcome responsibility supports the wider view of corrective justice,[31] we must note that the justification for imposing outcome responsibility on those who cause harm to others rests not on corrective but on distributive justice. Perry rightly points to the distinction

29. According to Jules Coleman, the implication of "harm" is that a legitimate interest of the plaintiff has suffered: see Coleman, *Tort Law and Demands*, above n.5, at p.350.
30. See below, question (5).
31. Wider in the sense that reasons other than fault may support a duty to compensate.

between outcome responsibility from the agent's point of view – something that helps him foster a sense of his personal identity, character and history – and outcome responsibility as a justification for holding people liable to others for the harmful outcome of their conduct.[32] But I do not agree with him that these two aspects of outcome responsibility are inconsistent. The argument for holding people responsible to others for harmful outcomes is that it is fair to make the person to whom the advantages will flow from a uncertain situation over which he has some control (or which he has chosen to enter into) bear the losses that may equally flow from that situation. It is fair to treat the agent as if he had made a bet on the outcome of his action. This argument, somewhat loosely expressed, tries to spell out what justice requires in situations of uncertainty. It is a familiar notion in legal and extra-legal contexts. For example, the person to whom the income of property or a business will accrue if it does well has normally also to bear the risk of loss if it does badly. In the law of sales, when the right to income or fruits normally passes to the buyer, the risk of deterioration or destruction normally passes to him as well.

Aristotle and other philosophers who have developed the theory of distributive justice do not expressly mention this principle of risk, no doubt because it has arisen mainly in legal contexts. But, despite appearances, the risk principle rests on a form of distributive justice.[33] Though this form of justice is generally concerned with the distribution of goods, it also covers the distribution of losses and burdens. For example, it applies to the incidence of taxation. The just distribution of burdens and losses among the members of a society requires that a criterion be found (say benefit or capacity) according to which they may fairly be allocated. There is no reason why the distribution of the *risk* of gains or losses in a situation of uncertainty should not equally be part of distributive justice. To be specific, we can speak of the just distribution of risks as risk-distributive justice. It might seem at first sight that this sort of justice is not distributive,

32. Perry, above n.17, at pp.490–1.

33. This is not to accept Nickel's argument that corrective justice applies only to the impairment of distributively just holdings of goods: see James W. Nickel, "Justice in Compensation", 18 *Wm. & Mary Law Rev.* 379, 381–3, 385–8 (1976) cf. Jules L. Coleman, "Justice and the Argument for No-Fault", 3 *Social Theory & Practice* 161, 174, 180, n.19 (1975) [hereafter *Argument for No-Fault*]. Corrective justice applies to actual holdings, whether or not those actual holdings in justice ought to be redistributed in whole or part to other members of the community.

because the benefit of success and the risk of failure fall on the same person, whereas distributive justice is concerned with the allocation of assets and burdens among all or many of the members of a community. But the risk principle is entirely general. It places on every member of the community the burden of bearing the risk that his conduct may turn out to be harmful to others, in return for the benefit to himself that will accrue should his conduct turn out as he plans. It distributes throughout society the risks of harm attributable to human conduct.

d. The Blend of Corrective and (Risk-) Distributive Justice

I therefore take corrective justice to be in one way distinct from distributive justice and in another dependent on it. It is distinct in the sense that the interests (holdings) that corrective justice protects need not be just from a distributive point of view. The filthy rich can appeal to corrective justice if their holdings are filched by the grinding poor. But to justify corrective justice involves appealing at a certain stage to the just *distribution of risk* in a society. In that respect corrective justice depends on distributive justice. Corrective justice is a genuine form of justice only because the just distribution of risks requires people of full capacity to bear the risk of being held responsible for harming others by their conduct even when they are not at fault in doing so.[34] For this reason, corrective justice is a substantive, not a merely formal principle. It needs, and can be given, a moral basis.

This principle of risk distribution has an intuitive appeal. It may rest on the sort of moral intuition that one cannot go behind; or it may be that deeper analysis will show that it turns on something more fundamental. At any rate, risk distribution serves to justify outcome responsibility, and outcome responsibility opens the door to imposing a duty of reparation in suitable cases, and so to corrective justice. This conclusion is welcome, since it puts some parts of tort liability on a morally sound basis. But it does so only when the defendant has personally infringed the plaintiff's rights. For it is only when this is the case, and the harm-sufferer sues the person who is outcome responsible for the harm, that corrective justice by itself justifies the

34. How far this responsibility should be translated into strict legal liability depends on the answers to questions (5) and (6) below.

claim.

In criminal law, the offender is nearly always held responsible for what he has done personally. Vicarious liability or, what comes to the same thing, the liability of corporations and other bodies for the conduct of their members, is exceptional. Tort liability is different. Many tort actions give effect to personal responsibility. But others follow a different pattern. They are brought, for example, against an employer for the act of an employee who, in working for him, has harmed the plaintiff. In that case, outcome responsibility and corrective justice do not serve to justify an action against the employer,[35] though they may justify one against the employee. Is some other justification available? The conventional reasons given for holding that the employer ought to bear the risk of loss within certain limits for the employee's harmful conduct are that the employer (a) has control over the business, including the work of employees, and (b) stands to profit from the employee's services. A combination of these reasons, it is generally thought, justifies us in imposing vicarious responsibility on the employer. As in outcome responsibility, the person who, in situation of uncertainty, has a degree of control over how it will turn out, and who stands to gain if it goes in his favour, must bear the risk that it will turn out to harm another. This reasoning appeals once more to a principle of justice based on risk distribution. The justification of tort liability is, as before, a combination of corrective and distributive justice. But distributive justice now appears at two points rather than one. It does so, first, to support the outcome responsibility of the employee and, second, to support the action against the employer, who has not personally harmed the plaintiff.

In the end, the justification of tort liability both against the harm-doer personally and against secondary defendants, such as employers held to be vicariously liable, rests on both corrective and (risk-) distributive justice.

35. Richard Wright argues that corrective justice requires the employer to compensate the victim "for injuries that are tortiously inflicted in pursuance of the employer's objectives": Wright, above n.3, at p.674, n.219. But, as he himself recognizes, *id.* at p.674, it is unjust to compel someone to be an insurer for the fault of another, unless he has undertaken to do so (or, I would add, the just distribution of risks requires him to do so). It seems a mere fiction to argue that the employee's act is really the employer's, or must be treated as such.

5. *Subject to what conditions may one who by his conduct has infringed the rights of another be required to pay compensation?*

The main questions are whether fault is, morally speaking, a necessary condition of tort liability, and whether modern conditions justify using loss spreading to support liability that may be out of proportion to the blameworthiness of a defendant's conduct. The second question is not strictly about the legal conditions of tort liability but about a background state of affairs that may be necessary if the pursuit of corrective justice by tort law is to be morally defensible. Both questions raise the issue of how far, if at all, corrective justice should be tempered by considerations of retributive justice.

a. Retributive Justice and Fault in Criminal Law

To begin with fault, there is no doubt that, however this complex notion is interpreted, it is in general a necessary condition of conviction for a criminal offence, at any rate for a serious offence for which imprisonment is possible. One reason is that the law's prohibitions are meant to guide the potential offender's choices. Their aim is to influence conduct and their sanctions are directed at those who choose to do what the law forbids, not those who do the forbidden action without choosing to do it. If, therefore, the defendant had no choice, but was compelled to act as he did, for example if he was forced to steal against his will, it cannot be said that he *disregarded* the prohibition. He contravened it but, since he did not disregard or defy it, he should not be subject to punishment.

But the focus on choice does not stop there. If, though not compelled, the offender did not intend to do the wrong that the law forbids, he again cannot be said to have defied the prohibition. For example, if he did not mean the victim he assaulted to die, or if, oddly, he did not realise that the woman with whom he was having intercourse did not consent to it, he cannot be said to have flouted the prohibition of murder or rape, though he may have defied some lesser prohibition, say of assault or sexual harassment.

This condition of punishment, that the offender should have flouted the law, by intentionally doing what it forbids, is well settled for serious cases that carry heavy penalties. This remains true though the offender, given the difficulties of proof and the desire not to reward ignorance of the law, need not have known the exact terms in which the prohibition is couched. When the wrongdoer's fault is less serious, say recklessness or negligence,[36] most legal systems will still permit lesser degrees of punishment. In these latter types of cases, the offender need not have deliberately flouted the prohibition. It is sufficient that he behaved in a way that displayed too much self-regard and too little concern for the interest of others. Indifference or unconcern, falling short of defiance, is enough. Moreover, when the penalty is only a modest fine, fault even in the sense of indifference or unconcern may be dispensed with altogether and strict liability imposed. Yet even in the case of strict liability, the defendant must have chosen to act as he did. Compulsion will exclude punishment. But given the element of choice, the case for punishment here depends on the just distribution of risks. The criminal law may properly be used to ensure that those who, acting in their own interest, create a risk to others should suffer a modest penalty for the harm that their activity brings about. For example, the seller of milk which, unknown to him, is adulterated may properly be fined a modest sum for selling adulterated milk. There is therefore in practice a rough correlation between the type of fault or conduct and the weight of the punishment imposed. For the most serious penalties the offender must have chosen to defy the law, for the somewhat less serious he must have chosen to act with indifference to the interests of others, and for the relatively minor he must at least have chosen to do something that is potentially harmful to others.

What has been said describes in outline the correlation between fault/conduct and penalty in most systems of criminal justice. Can this rough correlation be morally justified? It has a certain intuitive appeal. The principle on which it seems to rest is retributive. The retributive principle has, however, two aspects. One *requires* that a sanction be imposed that is roughly proportionate to the moral gravity of the conduct. The other *forbids* that a sanction be imposed that is out of proportion to the gravity of the conduct. It is this second, limiting, aspect of the retributive principle that is in play here. The limiting principle requires the sanction to be no greater than is justified by the

36. Offences of negligence such as negligent wounding and killing are of course commoner in civil law than common law systems, but they are by no means absent from the common law.

gravity of the conduct, of which the degree of fault is an important ingredient. Of course, the correlation is extremely rough.

It may be objected that talk of the retributive principle is out of place. According to some versions of retributive justice, there can be no punishment in the absence of fault, since conduct that is free from fault does not possess even a minor degree of moral gravity. Hence there should be no strict liability in criminal law. But a person who freely does something chooses to intervene in the world and, while what he does may display neither defiance of nor indifference to the interests of others, it may, in pursuit of his own interests, put others at risk. It seems reasonable to put conduct that exposes others to a risk that materializes – for example selling milk that may possibly be and in fact is adulterated – at a fairly low point on the scale of misconduct on which showing indifference to and defiance of the interests of others occupy the higher reaches. The behaviour located low on the scale is not morally bad, and does not amount to fault, but neither is it morally indifferent; conduct that may affect others cannot be that. It is taking a chance of harming others.[37] Suitably extended, therefore, the retributive principle can surely treat as just, and not merely expedient, the imposition of minor sanctions for risk-creating conduct that goes wrong. The retributive principle, thus modified, would still require the gravity of the conduct to be roughly proportionate to the sanction.

Of course, even without this suggested extension, retribution as a theory intended to justify the criminal process has been fiercely attacked. But it has its defenders so far as sentencing is concerned, and every system of criminal justice, so far as I know, pays some attention to it in that context. This is not the place for a detailed discussion of the case for it; I merely assume that, in its limiting form, it has some merit. And if it is right to require the conduct to be of sufficient moral gravity to correspond roughly to the severity of the penalty imposed in criminal law, something similar must in principle be true in tort law as well.

37. Stephen Perry says it is based on something resembling fault: see Perry, above n.17, at p.504. The difference is between what one should not in any case do and what one may do provided it does not turn out to be harmful to others.

b. Retributive Justice and Fault in Tort Law

How should the retributive principle apply in tort law? First, the tortfeasor, like the criminal offender, presumably ought not to be made to pay unless he has chosen to do what the law forbids. There should be no tort liability for an act done under compulsion. So much seems to be required by the fact that tort law, like criminal law, is meant to influence conduct by inducing people to abstain from undesirable behaviour. But, as tort law does not impose imprisonment, there is on the retributive principle no strong case for requiring that a tortfeasor should have intended to defy the law, though, if he did, the case for a sanction is strengthened.[38] Provided his behaviour was selfish or inconsiderate, which negligent conduct often is, he may properly be made liable in tort. But the burdens of tort liability, though less grave than losing one's physical freedom, can be very serious, especially if the defendant is not insured.[39] In such cases, the retributive principle will not merely justify but require fault as a condition of tort liability.

In other cases, however, fault will not be necessary. A tort defendant is often insured and in some of the commonest types of tort liability, such as motoring accidents, insurance is compulsory. Hence the defendant does not have to pay the damages personally, except to the extent that he pays them indirectly through his insurance premium. Provided that the insurance premium is modest, therefore, there seems no moral reason to require fault as a condition of liability in these cases.[40] In practice many countries, such as France and Germany, impose strict liability for transport accidents, relying on insurance to minimize the burden on individual defendants. Again, when the defendant is vicariously liable for the conduct of an employee,[41] the retributive principle may not require that his

38. See generally David G. Owen, "The Moral Foundations of Punitive Damages", 40 *Ala. Law Rev.* 705 (1989).

39. Or if his employer is vicariously liable for his conduct but exercises rights of subrogation against him – in practice a rare event.

40. See generally Coleman, *Argument for No-Fault*, above n.33, at pp.173–4; Jules Coleman, "Mental Abnormality, Personal Responsibility and Tort Liability", in *Mental Illness: Law and Public Policy* (ed. Baruch A. Brody and H. Tristram Engelhardt, Jr., 1980) pp.107, 118–21, 123–4. Cf. Jules Coleman, "The Morality of Strict Liability", 18 *Wm. and Mary Law Rev.* 259, 283–4 (1976).

41. For whose conduct the employer properly bears the risk according to principles of distributive justice.

liability be confined to cases where the employee is at fault. Since the profit that falls to the employer is not always merely the amount that he deserves to make, but may include windfalls, an employer's vicarious liability need not be confined to accidents caused by fault on the part of the employee, but may sometimes extend to harm that is purely accidental.[42]

Often, therefore, there should in principle be no moral objection to strict liability in tort law,[43] provided that it does not impose an undue burden on the defendant personally. Hence it is not surprising that the degree of care and skill required in tort law is a stringent one. The standard of negligence is nearly always objective. The defendant may therefore be held liable for faults that a reasonable person would not have committed but that he could not help because he was too rash, clumsy or stupid.[44] Though nominally the liability is for fault, the defendant is in effect subject to strict liability. Of course, often fault is actually present, but the faults in question may be rather minor ones of inattention and slowness to react.

What has been said so far shows that corrective justice as tempered by the retributive principle supports some strict liability, but not universal strict liability. But it also shows that the line between fault and strict liability is often blurred. And even when fault is genuinely a condition of tort liability, and still more when liability is objective or strict, the compensation payable may be disproportionate to what is often a minor fault. To avoid this disproportion, the retributive principle insists that defendants should not be exposed to disproportionately heavy losses. If the claims of corrective justice are to be morally viable, ways must therefore be found of spreading such losses

Insurance provides a mechanism for spreading losses, and helps at the same time to protect the plaintiff's claim to compensation. Loss spreading is indeed often achieved by a form of distributive justice that allocates burdens roughly in proportion to benefits. Those who benefit from some activity, say motoring, are made to bear a proportionate share of the losses that the activity causes, for example

42. It is true that in practice legal systems tend to confine vicarious liability of employers to accidents attributable to employee fault.

43. As Coleman has pointed out, the retributive arguments in favour of fault liability in tort law as it operates in practice are rather weak: *Argument for No-Fault*, above n.33, at pp.162–72. But see David G.Owen, "The Fault Pit", 26 *Ga. Law Rev.* 703 (1992).

44. Above pp. 16–17, 24.

through compulsory third-party insurance. This is certainly not an infallible instrument of justice, since insurance premiums may be exorbitant. Nevertheless, it helps to ensure that tort damages are in most cases not grossly disproportionate to the fault of the defendant who has caused the harm. Hence, though loss spreading (through third-party insurance) is distributive, the reason why it is needed as an adjunct to the tort system is, in part at least, to satisfy the demands of retributive justice. It serves to cushion losses which, whether the defendants are at fault or not, are out of scale with the gravity of their conduct. This does not entail that loss spreading is an aim of the tort system as such, merely that it is essential if a system of corrective justice is to operate fairly in modern conditions. Corrective justice can operate as a morally defensible system only in harness with retributive justice. This in turn may require recourse to a form of justice that distributes burdens equitably.

So, while corrective justice in isolation warrants holding people strictly liable to make good the loss to those whom they harm without justification, the tort system is not bound to translate this into a legal liability to compensate, when to do so would be unduly burdensome to the defendant. On the contrary, the retributive principle requires that the burden be made roughly proportionate to the gravity of the conduct. In many instances this can to some extent be achieved by making fault a condition of liability. In others, the personal burden on the defendant must be reduced, whether he is at fault or not, by a system that redistributes losses among those who benefit from the activities that cause them. In that way full compensation can be achieved, as corrective justice demands, provided that the personal liability of the defendant is tempered by loss distribution.

6. *What limits should be placed on the amount of compensation payable?*

Retributive and distributive justice are not the only moral considerations that may limit the untrammelled pursuit of corrective justice. Three other reasons are commonly given for restricting the compensation payable in tort actions: the scope of the rule violated, the foreseeability of the harm for which compensation is sought, and the conduct of the plaintiff. A fourth is more radical. It is sometimes said that tort liability should be replaced, entirely or above a certain amount, by a state compensation scheme, at least in certain areas of life.[45] What is the moral status of these arguments?

a. The Scope of the Rule Violated

A rule making conduct tortious, for example requiring dangerous machinery to be fenced, may have a limited scope. It may be that, properly interpreted, the aim of the rule is to prevent parts of the employee's body or clothes catching in the machinery rather than to prevent parts of the machinery flying out and injuring someone. There is nothing special to tort law about this need for interpretation. Every rule that makes conduct wrongful, whether in criminal law, tort law, the law of contract, trust law or whatever, requires interpretation and the interpretation will set limits to the scope of the rule in question. When the interpretation excludes certain types of harm, the pursuit of corrective justice by the use of state machinery is to that extent ruled out. But is it just to exclude, for example, certain of the plaintiff's economic, psychological or emotional interests from the scope of a tort law rule or from tort law as a whole?

It seems that the state must be justified in imposing some limits on the type of harm for which compensation may be claimed. To require compensation for every type of harm in the context of every rule of tort law would to be impose a burdensome liability on defendants. It would be inefficient when, as is likely to be the case with some types of harm difficult to ascertain, the cost of imposing tort liability would much exceed the likely benefit. The legislature and courts must be entitled to take the view that some interests – say, wrongfully inflicted but trivial psychological harm – do not deserve the status of a right. Of course, the state may make mistakes in these matters, but it must surely be justified, indeed bound, to mark out such limits on liability. If the state is bound to decide what conduct should be made criminal or tortious, fallible as its judgment may be, it must also be bound to fix the limits of responsibility for various types of harm.

b. The Foreseeability of the Harm

The foreseeability of the harm for which compensation is claimed is often put forward, particularly in tort claims based on negligence, as an independent ground for limiting the extent of the defendant's liability. The ground for this limitation is sometimes said to be that,

45. As in New Zealand, with respect to accidents.

when the liability is based on negligently failing to foresee and take steps to avoid harm, the resulting liability should logically be restricted to the harm, or type of harm, that should have been foreseen. Thus, if the defendant should have foreseen harm by impact alone, he should not be liable for the harm by fire or explosion that unexpectedly results. This argument assumes that there is never a case for placing the risk of an unexpected outcome on the person at fault in creating the risk.[46] The argument is no more convincing than the view that, where it is a condition of liability that the defendant intended harm, the harm for which he is liable should be confined to what he intended. The conditions of liability (question (5) above) and the extent of liability (this question (6)) present somewhat different moral and policy issues. But the retributive principle does require a rough proportion to be preserved between the degree of fault and the burden of the sanction. To rule out recovery for unforeseeable harm, or harm of an unforeseeable type, enables courts to limit the extent of the burden, though in a somewhat arbitrary way given the fluidity of the criteria used to identify unforeseeable harm after the event. But it must be stressed that the argument for proportionality weakens when the defendant does not pay the compensation personally, as in cases of insured, vicarious and organizational liability, which bulk large in tort liability for negligence.

c. Conduct and Fault of the Plaintiff

Corrective justice suggests that the defendant's duty to compensate the plaintiff should be limited when the plaintiff's conduct, along with that of the defendant, is a cause of the harm. In that case the plaintiff as well as the defendant is responsible for the outcome. If they are both responsible the plaintiff should bear part of the loss himself. How great that part should be will depend on whether causal contribution can be quantified. The question is controversial, though in my view the notion of causal contribution is a coherent one.[47] If causal contribution can be assessed, the plaintiff's claim, from the viewpoint of corrective justice, should be reduced proportionately to

46. Hart and Honoré, above n.28, at pp.259–75.
47. Hart and Honoré, above n.28, at pp.225–35.

that contribution. If not, retributive principles must be taken into account.

Suppose that the plaintiff's conduct has not merely been a cause of the harm along with the conduct of the defendant, but that the plaintiff has been at fault in behaving as he did, or has acted with deliberation. Should the plaintiff's fault or deliberation bar or reduce his compensation? The plaintiff may be morally disentitled to sue, for instance because he consented to the defendant's conduct or intentionally provoked it. More difficult is the question how far his recovery should be affected by the fact that, short of intentional provocation, his fault contributed to the harm done. Does the existence of contributory fault modify the claim to compensation on the basis of corrective justice? To reduce the plaintiff's claim from what corrective justice on its own would warrant is to impose a loss on him. The retributive principle requires the loss to be not disproportionate to his fault. This sets a limit to the possible extent of the reduction, but does not settle the question whether a reduction proportionate to fault is morally required. If both plaintiff and defendant were at fault in causing the harm, the straightforward retributive principle would make both plaintiff and defendant responsible to an extent roughly proportionate to the gravity of their respective faults. Putting these considerations together, the plaintiff's claim, when both he and defendant are at fault, should be reduced by an amount that results in plaintiff and defendant bearing a share of the loss roughly proportionate to their respective faults, but not so as to impose on the plaintiff a loss disproportionate to his fault considered in isolation. In practice, those legal systems that admit the apportionment of damages for contributory negligence adopt these criteria, or something rather like them.

d. The Replacement of Tort Liability by a State Scheme of Compensation

According to Richard Wright, the replacement of tort liability by a compulsory no-fault state compensation scheme would be inconsistent with corrective justice.[48] It would fail to impose the duty to compensate on the party who ought to bear it and impose it on persons who, from the point of view of corrective justice at least, have no duty

48. Wright, above n.3, at p.704.

to bear it. The effect of such a scheme is to transfer the whole or part of the duty to compensate from the harm-doer to the taxpayer or the contributors to an insurance fund.

There is, however, an argument for doing precisely this, based on the just distribution of risks. If it is fair for everyone to have to contribute through taxes to the defence of the country, since everyone in the country benefits from its being defended, so it is fair for everyone who owns or drives a vehicle, or who benefits from the existence of a transport system, to contribute to the accident costs that such a system carries with it. To argue in this way is simply to extend to a wider group the sort of argument that leads to an employer being held liable for the harm done by his employee when engaged in working for him. Of course there is a technical difference in that, under the imagined state scheme, the harm-doer would not be liable in tort, while in the law of vicarious liability as it stands in most countries, the employee remains liable even when his employer is vicariously liable. But in practice the employee is not sued, because he will usually not be able to pay the damages, or not so easily as the employer, and usually he does not even pay the insurance premium that covers the employer's potential liability for his harmful conduct. It would hardly be an injustice to take from the harm-sufferer (who is entitled to compensation from another source) a technical right to sue the harm-doer.

That is not to say that there is a morally compelling case for replacing tort liability by a state compensation scheme. To do so would tend to undermine the sense of personal responsibility of some potential harm-doers, just as vicarious liability tends to undermine the sense of personal responsibility of some employees. But to introduce a state compensation scheme would not in my view violate corrective justice. The propriety of corrective justice depends, I have argued, on our taking a certain view about the just distribution of risks in a society, a view for which individual outcome responsibility provides a basis. But it is possible to take a wider view about how risk should be distributed, at least in certain areas of life. One can argue that the distribution of risks should, for example as regards motoring, take place at the level not of the individual but of the vehicle-owning population or the whole community. The level at which risks should be distributed in a particular area of community life seems pre-eminently a matter of political judgment.

3. The Answers Summarized

A brief summary of the suggested answers to the six questions discussed may be helpful:

(1) and (2) By the tort system the state aims to reduce the incidence of undesirable conduct by treating certain individual interests as rights, and giving the right-holder the power to protect his rights and obtain compensation if they are infringed by undesirable conduct marked as a civil wrong.

(3) The state is justified in maintaining, and probably in subsidizing, a tort system and an institutional framework, including courts, to give effect to it.

(4) Subject to (5) and (6) below, tort-plaintiffs in principle are morally entitled, on the basis of corrective justice, to recover damages from tort-defendants who have without justification personally caused them harm. On a wide view, corrective justice requires those who have without justification harmed others by their conduct to put the matter right, even if they were not at fault. The reason is that we are responsible for the outcome of our conduct (outcome responsibility), and that a just distribution of risks requires us to make good the harm our conduct causes to others in return for the benefit and credit that accrues to us when our plans come off. The case for imposing vicarious liability in tort on employers and organizations who have not personally caused the harm also rests on the just distribution of risks.

(5) But the pursuit of corrective justice must be tempered by the need to keep a proportion between the burden of compensation that falls on a defendant personally and the gravity of his conduct. There are cases in which it is unjust to hold the defendant liable in the absence of fault and in which, even if he is at fault, the extent of his personal liability should be limited by loss spreading. The moral basis of the need for proportionality is the retributive principle, which requires that the sanction should not be disproportionate to the gravity of the conduct for which it is imposed. The argument for proportionality does not apply, or applies more weakly, when the liability is vicarious rather than personal.

(6) The pursuit of corrective justice is also tempered by the duty and power of the state to decide which harms are to count as infringing legal rights. The state is justified in reducing or refusing compen-

sation when the harm lies outside the scope of the rule of law on which the plaintiff relies, or was of an unforeseeable type the risk of which should not be imposed on the defendant. When the plaintiff's conduct contributes to the harm he suffers, the extent to which his claim should be reduced, if any, should be settled according to the principles of corrective justice and the retributive principle. Lastly, it would not be unjust, though it might be unwise, for the state to replace tort liability in certain areas by a scheme of no-fault insurance based on the just distribution of losses. The principle of corrective justice that justifies the straightforward cases of tort liability, in which the defendant has personally done the harm, has therefore to be tempered by considerations of distributive and retributive justice that limit the extent to which it can properly be applied.

5

NECESSARY AND SUFFICIENT CONDITIONS IN TORT LAW[1]

Argument about causation inside and outside the law is often concerned with the question: must a cause be a *necessary* condition, or a *sufficient* condition of a result, or must it be a *necessary element in a set of conditions jointly sufficient* to produce the result? This essay supports the third view both outside the law and inside it, whenever a sequence of physical events is in issue. A different but related idea can be used to explain reasons for human action, "causing" or inducing people to act rather than causing things to happen. There is, I contend, no special legal meaning of causation and the related concepts such as inducement.

On the other hand, law alone determines when causal connection must be proved and when it can be dispensed with in legal contexts. When causal connection must be proved, law also settles what must be shown to have caused what. This is specially important in tort law. Tort law generally imposes fault liability on people who by their wrongful conduct cause harm to others; but sometimes it imposes strict liability on people who engage in activities which, though not wrongful, cause others harm. The causal inquiry takes a different form according as fault or strict liability is in issue.

Tort lawyers have traditionally held the view that, whatever the meaning of causal connection, the way to test whether it exists in a given case is to ask whether in the circumstances the harmful result would have occurred in the absence of the wrongful act. This is to adopt the but-for test, by which causal connection exists between condition and consequence whenever, but for the condition, the consequence would not in the circumstances have occurred. The but-for

1. First published in *Philosophical Foundations of Tort Law* (ed. David G. Owen, Oxford 1995) pp.363–85.

test is also called the test of strong necessity.[2] It often gives what is intuitively the right answer, but sometimes fails to do so. This test is meant to exclude those factors that had no impact on a particular course of events. But sometimes it cuts out factors that did have an impact. It serves to exclude many irrelevant conditions, but also excludes others that are relevant.[3] Thus in some cases of over determination – cases where two or more independent wrongful acts alone would have sufficed to bring about the harm – the but-for test leads to the dubious conclusion that neither act caused the harm. So, if the but-for test were applied to such a case, the victim could recover from neither wrongdoer. As a way around this and other difficulties, courts have developed an alternative test of causal connection, for use in tort cases when the but-for test seems to give the wrong answer. This alternative test asks whether the condition in question was a "substantial" factor in producing the result. But this device, which allows judges and juries to follow their intuitions, is purely pragmatic[4] and leaves the theoretical problem untouched. The substantial factor notion is indefinite, if not indeterminate, and it is difficult to see how it might be fitted into a coherent theory of causation.

1. The Causation Story: Modern Efforts to Unravel its Mysteries

In 1959 Herbert Hart and I proposed a thesis that we thought would explain the basis of and justify our intuitions in certain unusual cases, such as the over-determination situation, as well as straightforward ones.[5] We argued that, to be a cause of an event, a prior event must be shown to be a causally relevant condition of that event. Whether something more is needed to turn a causally relevant condition into a cause may for the moment be left aside; for now let it be assumed

2. On strong and weak necessity and sufficiency see John L. Mackie, *The Cement of the Universe: A Study of Causation* pp.39–40, 60–6, 126–7 (1974); Richard W. Wright, "Causation, Responsibility, Risk, Probability, Naked Statistics and Proof: Pruning the Bramble Bush by Clarifying the Concepts" [hereafter *Pruning*] 73 *Iowa Law Rev.* 1001, 1020 (1988).
3. Wright, *Pruning*, above n.2, at p.1022.
4. Id. at pp.1018–19.
5. H.L.A. Hart and A.M. Honoré, *Causation in the Law* (1959).

(contrary to our view) that every causally relevant condition is a cause. Our theory was that an event such as a prior wrongful act is causally relevant only if it is a necessary element in a set of conditions that is together sufficient to produce the consequence.

> "A condition may be necessary just in the sense that it is one of a set of conditions jointly sufficient for the production of the consequence. It is necessary because it is required to complete this set".[6]

At least that was true, we said, of physical sequences.[7] This weak sense of "necessary" (necessary to that particular set of conditions) can be contrasted with the strong necessity inherent in the but-for test. On the other hand our sense of "sufficient" is a strong one. If the set of conditions sufficient to produce the consequence occurred, the consequence occurred; and if the consequence had not occurred, the set of conditions would not have occurred either.[8]

In 1965 John Mackie had applied our idea to causal regularities – causal generalizations rather than specific events.[9] He combined with it the doctrine of the plurality of causes. This latter theory postulates that on different occasions certain types of events – say death or road accidents – can have different causes. We discover causal regularities, and ultimately scientific causal laws, by assembling sets of conditions. Ideally these should be such that we can say of a condition that it is a necessary[10] member of a set such that, when all the members of the set are present, the consequence invariably follows. The conditions are jointly sufficient for the result but, in view of the plurality of causes, they may not actually be necessary for it, since there may be alternative sets of conditions that will also produce the same consequence.[11] Mackie called such a condition – a necessary member of a set jointly sufficient (but unnecessary) to produce a given type of

---

6. Id. at p.106. A different, though related account was needed for interpersonal transactions.
7. H.L.A. Hart and Tony Honoré, *Causation in the Law* (2nd ed. 1985) pp.51–61, 125. See below, nn.59–61 and accompanying text.
8. This is to apply the reverse but-for test. Wright, *Pruning*, above n.2, at p.1021 n.108. Richard Wright termed a condition of this sort, necessary in a weak sense but sufficient in a strong sense, a "NESS" condition. He derived it from the NESS test, which is meant to replace the but-for test: id. at 1019. See below, nn.16 and 17 and accompanying text.
9. Mackie, above n.2, at pp.59–63 (building to some extent on Konrad Marc-Wogau, "On Historical Explanation", 28 *Theoria* 213–33 (1962)).
10. Mackie says insufficient (on its own), which is obvious, but also non-redundant, i.e. necessary as an element in that particular jointly sufficient set of conditions: *id.* p.62.
11. I have modified his terminology so far as the use of "factor" and "condition" are concerned.

result – an INUS (Insufficient but Necessary part of an Unnecessary but Sufficient) condition.

For example, there may be one causal regularity, by which a driver's not keeping a proper lookout plus certain other conditions is sufficient to bring about a road accident, and another causal regularity, by which going too fast plus a different set of conditions is sufficient for a road accident. If so, not keeping a proper lookout and going too fast are both INUS conditions of road accidents, though, belonging to different sets,[12] neither condition is necessary to produce a road accident.

It is worth noting that sets of conditions of this sort generally have as one of their members the absence of counteracting or frustrating conditions. A certain dose of strychnine will, given certain bodily conditions, result in death, but only (1) in the absence of an antidote and (2) in the absence of some other cause of death intervening before the poison takes effect. The strength of the dose, the bodily conditions and the absence of an antidote, the absence of some other intervening cause of death etc. are all INUS members of the set of conditions that is together sufficient to result in death.

With some hesitation[13] Mackie concluded that though this analysis of causal regularities as sets of INUS conditions often applies not only to types of event but to specific events,[14] it does not always do so.[15] He thought that at least sometimes we can say of a specific instance of a condition, such as not keeping a proper lookout, that it caused a collision, though we are not thereby committed to any regularity that would make not keeping a lookout an INUS condition of road accidents. It was not just that we and scientific experts are unable to frame a satisfactory generalization combining speed, position of the victim, visibility, road condition etc. in the right proportions. Rather we sometimes conclude that, but for the lack of a proper lookout, *this* collision would not have occurred without believing even in principle that this was an instance of a regularity concerning speed, position, road condition and the other factors. "A singular causal

12. They could also, of course, belong to the same set.
13. Mackie, above n.2, at pp.48–50 adduces powerful arguments for a cause as something necessary and sufficient in the circumstances for its effect. Cf. Wright, *Pruning*, above n.2, at pp.1028–9.
14. Mackie, above n.2, at pp.65–6.
15. *Id.* pp.40–58.

statement need not imply even the vaguest generalization".[16] If in a specific case we can back our conviction up by pointing to a set of INUS conditions, so much the better; but that is not essential.

In 1985 Richard Wright in an important paper dissented from Mackie's view on this point and, propounding the NESS (Necessary Element of a Sufficient Set) test, elaborated the idea that Hart and I had originally put forward.[17] His version is only marginally different from ours. According to Wright

> "a particular condition was a cause of (contributed to) a specific result if and only if it was a necessary element of a set of antecedent actual conditions that was sufficient for the occurrence of the result".[18]

This perhaps differs from our view in one respect. Wright seems to require that all the conditions that belong to the set be antecedent to the result, whereas it appears to me that, to be sufficient for the result, some conditions at least can be of the sort that must persist until the result occurs. An example is the icy condition of the road as a factor in a road accident.

This difference of view, if it is one, does not affect the value of the NESS test, which is widely supported by tort theorists, and not only by them.[19] Nevertheless Mackie is not alone in defending the but-for notion as an analysis of singular causal statements. In German criminal law Friedrich Toepel has recently published a monograph on crimes of negligence, which clearly have much in common with tort actions. Toepel supports the but-for test and dissents from the dominant view among German scholars, which rejects it.[20]

The controversy is clearly not over. In sections 2 and 3, I explore some aspects of causal connection that are common to the NESS and but-for theories and others that divide them. The analysis focuses in particular on how far causation in tort law depends on concepts that

---

16. Mackie, above n.2, at pp. 77–8, effectively criticized by Wright, *Pruning*, above n.2, at pp.1031–4.
17. Richard Wright, "Causation in Tort Law" 73 *Cal. Law Rev.* 1735 (1985) (especially pp.1788–1813) [hereafter *Causation*]; Wright, *Pruning*, above n.2, at pp.1018–44.
18. Wright, *Pruning*, above n.2, at p.1019 n.98.
19. See Wright, *id.* p.1019 n.98. For a criminal law example see Ingeborg Puppe, "Der Erfolg und seine kausale Erklärung im Strafrecht", 92 *ZStW* 863, 867f (1980); "Die Beziehung zwischen Sorgfaltswidrigkeit und Erfolg bei den Fahrlässigkeitsdelikten" 99 *ZStW* 595–6 (1987).
20. F. Toepel, *Kausalität und Pflichtwidrigkeitszusammenhang beim fahrlässigen Erfolgsdelikt* (1992).

apply outside the law, and how far it reflects normative considerations, legal or moral.

2. Common Elements in the NESS and But-For Theories

Some points are, or should be, common ground between the NESS and but-for theories. First, each of these theories embraces both a search for the *meaning* of "causally relevant condition" and a *test* by which we can tell whether a condition is causally relevant. That is, they are both at times semantic and at times heuristic. The importance of the distinction is that we may believe that a condition was a cause of a specific event because it was a member of a set of conditions jointly sufficient to bring it about and yet not be able to say exactly what those conditions were. We may therefore mean by cause a condition of that sort, and yet be satisfied in a given instance that it was a cause on the basis of the rough uniformities observed in everyday life that lead us to think that the presence of the condition made a difference to the outcome. We may do this though we could not specify the INUS conditions that are exemplified in the case in hand.[21] No one will deny that the but-for test has in many instances a heuristic value: it often provides a quick way of testing the existence of causal connection. It is another matter whether it is part of the *meaning* of "causally relevant condition" or "cause".

Philosophers debate whether causal connection is a relation between events or between facts.[22] An event can be described in many different ways but a fact is tied to a specific description. That Brutus stabbed Caesar and that he betrayed Caesar describe the same historical *event* but the fact that Brutus stabbed the dictator is not the same *fact* as the fact that he betrayed him. This difference has a bearing on what a plaintiff must prove in a lawsuit. In a wrongful death action by Caesar's widow, she would have to prove, first, the fact that Brutus stabbed her husband and, second, the further fact that Caesar's death was caused by the first fact of Brutus' stabbing; it would not be enough to show that Brutus betrayed Caesar, even though what Brutus did could be truthfully described as betrayal, because not all forms of betrayal will found tort actions.

21. But see Mackie, above n.2, at pp.54–5, expressing the contrary view.
22. Mackie, above n.2, at pp.248–265.

In my view both events and facts can be causally connected; and in law, including tort law, both events and facts can be relevant. A plaintiff must (1) identify the event or events that give rise to the claim and (2) prove that the fact that the defendant acted in a certain way caused the harm of which he complains. He must point to the time, place and persons involved, which can be described in many different ways. But he must go on to show that some specific aspect of the events he identifies (such as the fact that the defendant drove at an excessive speed) brings the defendant within the relevant legal category, and supports the conclusion that his wrongful or risk-creating conduct caused the harm of which the plaintiff complains. He must show that the element that makes the conduct wrongful or creates the undue risk was relevant to the harmful outcome for which the law provides a remedy.

Thus, if the plaintiff alleges that the defendant drove at excessive speed, he must show that the fact that he drove at that such-and-such a speed rather than at the proper speed was relevant to the fact that the plaintiff suffered such-and-such injuries. Though the incident in which the defendant is alleged to have driven at an excessive speed can be described in different ways – as Dan Dawes driving down Main Street, or as the engineer in the yellow Jersey hurrying to get home – these descriptions serve merely to identify the incident in issue. Again, if the plaintiff injured in an explosion relies on strict liability for the defendant's use of explosives, he must show that the fact that the defendant used explosives was relevant to the damage for which he seeks redress, though what the defendant did can be described in various other ways – quarrying for stone, or trying out a new fuse. Law is so structured that a plaintiff must prove a connection between the facts that specify those features of the events that are both causally relevant and legally relevant in other ways.

It follows that the law determines the way in which the causal inquiry is framed. Causal connection (in German terminology *Kausalzusammenhang*) cannot be separated in cases of fault liability from unlawful connection (*Rechtswidrigkeitszusammenhang*); their separation in the writings of some German theorists is in my view a source of error. The inquiry is into whether certain faulty conduct (or risk-creating conduct entailing strict liability) caused certain harm. In a country where liability for driving an automobile depends on negligence, the legal issue will be whether the fact that the defendant *drove negligently* (e.g. without keeping a proper lookout) caused the injuries. But in a jurisdiction where automobile liability is strict, the question will be whether the fact that the defendant *drove* caused the harm. The answer to these two questions may be different. The defendant's driving may have caused the injury, yet his negligent driving may not have done so, because his negligence made no difference to the outcome; the same collision would have occurred had he driven carefully. In tort law, the issue is not the open-ended one "What caused this harm?" but "Did the fact that the defendant behaved in a certain unlawful or undue risk-creating way cause it?" The first question calls for an explanation of how the harm came about, the second for an assessment of the defendant's responsibility for conduct described in categories fixed by the law.

A good illustration is the case involving the navigation of a ship by an officer who was competent and experienced but who did not possess the certificate required by law.[23] The officer navigated negligently and the ship was involved in a collision. The defendants admitted that the negligent navigation caused the collision, but denied that the lack of a certificate was causally relevant. Had it been relevant the amount of damages would have been greater. Given that the basis of liability was fault, it was rightly held that the lack of a certificate was irrelevant, since the officer would have navigated no better had he possessed one.

The lack of a certificate would, it seems to me, have been causally relevant had it been the case that the officer was incompetent and that, in order to obtain a certificate, he would have had to acquire the necessary competence. On the other hand, had there been strict liability for navigating the ship without a certificate, so that if the ship was navigated by a pilot without a certificate the navigation was at the defendants' risk, the navigation would have been held to have caused the collision. Since strict liability is liability not for wrongful conduct, but for engaging in risk-creating activity, there would have been no need in this case to show that the lack of a certificate was causally relevant. In such a strict liability case, it would have been enough that, had the ship not been navigated by X (who did not in fact possess a certificate), no collision would have occurred. In the actual case, however, what explained the collision was the fact that the ship was negligently

23. *The Empire Jamaica* [1955] P. 52, 57–8.

navigated, not that it was navigated. There is a distinction between conduct that counts as a cause in an explanatory inquiry, on the one hand, and conduct that is made by the law a basis of liability provided it is causally connected with the harm suffered, on the other.

This point is misunderstood by Wright,[24] who thinks that the Hart and Honoré criteria of voluntary human action and abnormality (in the sense of actions and events that are unusual in the context), used to distinguish causes from mere causally relevant conditions, are meant to identify tortious conduct.[25] We are said to have difficulty in accommodating strict liability, where the conduct on which liability is based (e.g. using explosives) may not be either abnormal or voluntary in the sense of intended to do harm. But the role of our criteria is to mark a backward limit in explanatory causal inquiries, and only a forward limit to whatever responsibility is appropriate under other, normative, concepts of tort law. Our causal criteria are not a substitute for the other principles of tort law that define what conduct is wrongful or entails strict liability. That depends on positive law, and varies from system to system, some systems imposing strict liability or no liability in circumstances where others insist on fault (e.g. for auto accidents). It remains true, however, that often the law for good reason designates conduct as wrongful when it is intended to do harm or is a departure from a recognized norm. In this way wrongful conduct that causes harm often coincides with what would count as a causal explanation of the harm that ensues. But in cases of strict liability, where the wrongfulness of the defendant's conduct is not in issue, there is no occasion to trace a causal path from wrongfulness to the plaintiff's harm.

A third point is that, whichever theory we adopt, a hypothetical question must be put and answered. This involves a counterfactual proposition, namely that if a condition that in fact occurred had not occurred, the outcome would have been so-and-so.[26] On the but-for theory we must ask whether in the circumstances the consequence would have occurred had the condition not occurred. On the NESS theory we must ask whether in the circumstances the condition was a necessary member of a set of conditions that was together sufficient

24. Wright, *Pruning*, above n.2, at p.1014.
25. They are, we argue, meant to identify the *limits* of responsibility in most cases: Hart and Honoré (2nd ed.), above n.6, at pp.68–81.
26. Wright, *Pruning*, above n.2, at pp.1039–42.

to produce the consequence, i.e. would the remaining set of conditions have produced the consequence in the absence of the condition in issue?

But to speak of the absence of a condition, or the hypothesis that it did not occur, can mislead. It suggests that the condition we are interested in can be notionally eliminated and that we can then calculate what would have happened if only the remaining circumstances had been present. Wright says that we hypothetically eliminate the condition being tested without adding or subtracting any other conditions.[27] This view of elimination also has adherents in German legal theory, partly because theorists there tend to separate causal connection from unlawful connection. If this were the right way to test a causal hypothesis, we should indeed be comparing the real world with an imaginary world. For in the real world conduct is often a choice between alternatives. If John had not done so-and-so, he would have done something else. If he had not intervened, someone else would have, perhaps in a different way. Sometimes these alternatives would have had a bearing on the course of events we are investigating. Mackie rightly says that both necessity in the strong sense and sufficiency in the strong sense (viz. both the but-for and NESS theories) "involve assertions about how the world would have run on if something different had been done".[28]

But this is rather loosely expressed, for it leaves open the question "what is the something different that we must suppose to have been done"?[29]In many contexts the answer is "whatever would in the circumstances have occurred had the condition in question not occurred". Sometimes there is no reason to suppose that anything causally relevant would have occurred in that event, and then it looks as if the condition in issue is simply being eliminated as causally irrelevant. John dropped a lighted match on some brushwood. Did he cause the destruction of the forest? To test this, ask whether if John had not dropped the lighted match, the forest fire would have occurred. We begin by supposing the contradictory of the condition viz. "John did not drop the lighted match". Often it is clear that, had he not dropped the match, whatever else would have happened

27. *Id.* pp.1041–1042.
28. Mackie, above n.2, at pp.51–2.
29. For the reasons given in the text Wright's view and that of David K. Lewis, *Counterfactuals* (1973) pp.72–7 are unsatisfactory.

would not have resulted in a fire. But the position would be different if we knew that, had John not dropped a match, David would have done so anyway. In that case, though John will indeed have destroyed the forest, he destroyed a forest that was anyhow doomed, and that may affect the forest owner's claim. However, there is usually no reason to suppose any such alternative event and therefore no need expressly to substitute anything for the condition eliminated.

But the notion that we do not substitute anything for the condition whose causal relevance we are testing is an illusion. Suppose we want to test the assertion that Churchill kept Britain in the war in 1940. Was the fact that he was Prime Minister the cause of Britain remaining in the war? Here we cannot eliminate Churchill without substituting another Prime Minister whose hypothetical conduct of affairs would have had a bearing on whether Britain remained in the war. The contradictory of "Churchill was Prime Minister" viz. "Churchill was not Prime Minister" would have implied in the world of 1940 that someone else was Prime Minister (say Halifax); and we must then ask whether that person would have wanted and been able to convince Parliament and the British people to continue the war. The causal statement about Churchill implicitly contrasts him with this hypothetical substitute. It is true that logically "Churchill was not Prime Minister in 1940" is compatible with there being no Prime Minister at all. But it is the real world, not an imaginary world or a logical calculus, that determines what is implied in the context by the contradictory of the condition in question, and what should therefore be substituted for it in testing the counterfactual proposition. In that real world, had Churchill not been Prime Minister, someone else would have held that office. And that someone else might or might not have kept Britain in the war.

In a legal context the same approach may be applied, except that when the inquiry concerns the causal relevance of *wrongful* conduct, as is usual in tort claims, we must substitute for the wrongful conduct of the defendant *rightful* conduct on his part.[30] When liability is based on fault the comparison is not with what would have happened had the defendant done nothing, but with what would have happened had he acted properly. The reason for making this substitution is similar to that

30. Hart and Honoré (2nd ed.), above n.7, at pp.lviii–lx, 411–14; Toepel, above n.20, at p.106.

in Churchill's case. The contradictory of "the defendant acted wrongfully" is "the defendant did not act wrongfully", and this is logically quite unspecific; for instance it is compatible with his doing nothing. Once more we must turn to the features of the real world – in this case, the world of positive tort law – which tells us that what is implied by his not acting wrongfully is his acting rightfully. The reason why this is the appropriate substitution is that the aim of the legal inquiry is to discover not whether the defendant's conduct as such made a difference to the outcome, but whether the fact that it was wrongful did so.

Again, tort law normally requires the plaintiff to show that the wrongful *aspect* of the defendant's conduct was causally connected with the harm.[31] To eliminate driving at an excessive speed therefore requires us to substitute for the excessive speed driving at a proper speed, and then to ask whether that would have led to the injuries that in fact occurred. Moreover, the hypothesis of rightful conduct involves supposing not merely that the defendant drove at a proper speed, but also that the likely consequences of his doing so be taken into account. For example, if the pedestrian who was run over would have seen the defendant's automobile coming in time to avoid it, had he been driving at a reasonable pace, this must be taken into account. In the same way if someone other than Churchill had been in office, his colleagues would have been less afraid of contradicting him, and this must be taken into account in answering the historical question about 1940. In most legal contexts, the hypothetical inquiry requires that all conditions be kept steady, except that we substitute rightful conduct and its likely consequences for the wrongful conduct of which the defendant is alleged to have been guilty.

In the context of strict liability, however, the inquiry is more like that in the dropped match case.[32] Substitution of lawful conduct is not possible and is not required in cases of strict liability, since the defendant's conduct, though it creates a risk, is not unlawful unless it causes harm. In such a case the hypothetical inquiry thus must be

31. This is not the case if the law provides that, if the defendant acts unlawfully, he acts at his risk. Then, as in cases of strict liability, it has only to be shown that his action was causally connected with the harm, not that the wrongful aspect of it was so connected. Hart and Honoré, *Causation* (2nd ed.), above n.7, at lx–lxi. And of course there are torts, such as trespass, in which harm need not be proved.

32. The dropped match incident might crop up in the context of negligence in tort law. In that case the comparison would be between what the defendant did and his exercising due care in regard to the match e.g. by putting it out before throwing it away.

whether the plaintiff would have suffered injury had the defendant not engaged in the activity (e.g. using explosives) that entails strict liability. There is normally no reason to suppose that, if the defendant had not used explosives for blasting, he or someone else would then and there have injured the plaintiff by some other means.

Both inside and outside the law, therefore, the purpose of the inquiry determines how we should frame the hypothesis to be tested. Tort law lays down what counts as wrongful conduct or conduct entailing strict liability and so what the plaintiff has to prove. It aims to protect people against wrongful infringement of their rights and exposure to undue danger. So, to ascertain whether an infringement has occurred, the wrongful conduct of the defendant must normally be compared with the notional rightful conduct that the plaintiff was entitled to expect in the circumstances. The question is, whether the difference between the wrongful conduct that occurred in the real world and the rightful conduct (together with its likely consequences) that we imagine as occurring, would have led to a different result in the hypothetical world that resembles the real world in all other respects. In the strict liability context, where the law protects against risks created by lawful conduct on the part of others, the causal inquiry is adapted to that aim.

Does the fact that in tort law we normally compare wrongful with rightful conduct show that the causal question is a normative question in disguise? It does not, for the inquiry into what would have occurred had the defendant obeyed a legal norm is no more normative than the question what would have occurred had the Prime Minister been someone other than Churchill. The answer to these causal inquires has no normative component. It remains the same, even if we suppose that it would have been better for Britain to make peace in 1940, or that it would be better, in order to combat overpopulation, for those who drive automobiles to drive blindfold.

There are those who think that counterfactual propositions cannot be true or false.[33] The tort process however assumes, in my view rightly, that they can be. We can often know what on a certain hypothesis would happen in the real world. We know that if we strike a match under certain conditions a flame will appear. The statement "if a match is struck under conditions XYZ a flame will appear" can

33. Mackie, above n.2, at p.54; Toepel, above n.20, at p.55.

be true or false and its truth value can be tested. Why not, also, "if a match had been struck . . . a flame would have appeared"? The only difference is that the proposition about the past can be verified only indirectly, on the assumption that in similar conditions similar results recur. This assumption cannot itself be verified, but unless it is well-founded we cannot rely on causal regularities or scientific laws. Of course we are often uncertain what would have happened on a given occasion had the defendant acted lawfully. Here, though the counterfactual statement "had X not done what he did Y would not have happened" is in principle true or false, we cannot tell for certain which it is. We must then have recourse to rules of law that instruct the judge or jury to go by the probabilities and, if necessary, to fall back on rules about the burden of proof.

3. NESS versus But-For: Differences in the Theories

I now turn to some of the examples that supporters of the NESS and but-for theories interpret differently. Some concern over-determination, others indeterminacy. Over-determination cases, it will be recalled, involve two or more independent acts each of which alone would have sufficed to bring about the harm. In such cases, the separate causal processes may be similar or different, and they may culminate in harm either at the same time or successively. When (1) similar causal processes culminate in harm at the same time the NESS and but-for theories point to different causal conclusions. But when (2) the causal processes are different or (3) one culminates in harm before the other, they point to the same causal conclusion. In cases of (4) causing or inducing people to act, neither theory is adequate, but the notion of sufficiency, in a modified form, explains why these are thought of as causal or quasi-causal relations.

A. Over-determination: Similar Causal Processes Culminating at the Same Time

Two similar causal processes may culminate in the same harm at the same time. Two shots, negligently but independently fired by A and B when out hunting, simultaneously hit C and destroy his left eye. Each shot was sufficient to do this without the other, and the effects of the two shots cannot be distinguished. Neither shot was necessary in the strong but-for sense, but each was necessary in the weak sense that it was a necessary member of a set of conditions together sufficient to destroy the sight of the victim's eye.[34] It would be counter-intuitive to hold that neither A nor B is responsible for the loss of C's eye. But is that because legal policy, or intuitions about responsibility, lead us to disregard the lack of causal connection between each shot and the loss of the eye?

Mackie, supporting the but-for theory, holds that when this type of over-determination is present the cause of the harm consists in the acts of A and B taken as a cluster.[35] In the absence of both acts C's eyesight would not have been lost. But it makes no sense, he thinks, to ask which was the cause. Perhaps not, but why need we ask which was *the* cause? Cannot each shot have been *a* cause of the loss of eyesight in a sense adequate both to explain what happened causally and to ascribe responsibility to A and B? It seems that, in Mackie's view, if A and B are held liable in tort or criminal law this must be based on a legal policy that overrides the lack of causal connection, or must rest on a special legal concept of cause. Indeed he says in one passage, "whatever our actual concept may be, it is obvious that we can construct causal concepts as we wish, which may be useful for particular purposes".[36] It is worth asking, therefore, whether in such cases of simultaneous over-determination lawyers resort to a special legal notion of cause.

Our concepts are tools shaped by the purposes for which we use them. Causation is used mainly for three purposes: to provide recipes, to explain events and to allot responsibility. Its roots probably lie in the first of these. Even non-human primates find recipes for what they want. To crack a nut, you need a stone of a certain size and weight and you must bring it down on the nut with a certain force. You learn to construct what your sophisticated cousins of a later age will call a set of conditions together sufficient to produce a given result, nut-cracking. Having assembled what seems to be a set of sufficient conditions, you whittle them down by eliminating those that trial and error show to be unnecessary. It turns out to be necessary that the stone be of a certain weight, that a certain degree of force be

34. Necessity in this weak sense is described above. See, above, text accompanying nn.5–8.
35. Mackie, above n.2, at p.47. See also Toepel, above n.20, at pp.71–2, 84.
36. Mackie, above n.2, at p.58.

employed and that the nutshell be not too thick, but unnecessary that the wind lie in a northerly direction or that the agent utter a blood-curdling whoop. The recipe is general, built up over time as instances accumulate and conditions are tested.

The discovery of conditions that are necessary members of a set sufficient to produce some result can be used to *explain* events as well as to bring them about. It can extend to events over which we have no control. We seek to discover the conditions of these events, perhaps in order to control similar events in future, or simply to understand how the universe works. The knowledge thus acquired may come in handy, but it may be pursued for its own sake. It can be used to trace the effects of natural events and inanimate forces. It can also be used to assign responsibility – social responsibility – to human beings for the outcome of their conduct.

For all these purposes – making recipes, explaining events and attributing responsibility – we can use the concept of the necessary members of a set of conditions together sufficient to produce a result of a given type, though we may not be able to specify or quantify all the conditions. This limited ability to specify conditions does not prevent our using causal ideas to explain events backwards in terms of previous events and conditions, or to allot responsibility for conduct forwards in terms of outcomes. These are not normative functions. It makes no difference whether the event to be explained, or the conduct to be assessed, is judged good or bad. It is tort law, not the concept of cause, that invites us to focus on the outcome of wrongful conduct.

What bearing has this on the problem of over-determination? The lesson is surely that the NESS test is not confined to the context of responsibility in general or tort law in particular. To revert to the two independent shots by A and B that put out C's eye, the acts of A and B each exemplify how to put C's left eye out, if that was, perhaps, the objective of snipers in a military campaign. Each also provides an explanation of C's loss of his left eye. Why, then, should not each provide a basis for assigning legal and moral responsibility to A and B? No recourse to legal policy, or to normative considerations, is needed to reach the conclusion that both A and B independently caused the harm to C. None of the purposes for which causal concepts are used requires us to adopt the but-for theory. There can be different recipes for attaining a given type of result, more than one of which is available on a given occasion. There can be different explanations of an event of a given type in terms of prior or concurrent conditions, more than one of which is present on a given occasion. To prevent the construction of a brick wall, one recipe is to withhold bricks, another to withhold mortar. If A withholds bricks and B independently withholds mortar and the wall is not built, or built on time, have not both A and B prevented its construction? We do not need a special "legal" concept of cause to deal with simultaneous over-determination by similar causal processes.

Toepel in the context of criminal law denies that either A or B is responsible for putting out C's left eye in a case like the shooting case.[37] Apart from pointing to the presumption of innocence, he argues that it is arbitrary to disregard B's shot when deciding whether A's was a necessary member of a set of conditions sufficient to produce the harm, and vice versa. The answer to this objection is that B's shot can be provisionally disregarded when we are considering the set of conditions of which A's shot is a member because that set *may* be sufficient without B's shot. The proper procedure in investigating the cause of a physical sequence of events is to assemble a set of conditions apparently sufficient to produce and hence explain the result. This we do in the light of what we know to be INUS conditions of results of that type.[38] But the set we provisionally assemble may contain some conditions that turn out to have been unnecessary for the result.

For example, the provisional set of conditions might consist of A's shot, the distance between A and C, the strength of the wind, the colour of A's jacket, and B's shot. We then reduce the set by eliminating those conditions that were not necessary to it. This disposes of the colour of A's jacket. B's shot we provisionally eliminate not because it was clearly not necessary, but because our knowledge of causal regularities and scientific laws leads us to think that A's shot *may* have been sufficient to put C's eye out without B's. Having reduced the set so far, we then test the relevance of A's shot (more precisely the fact that A shot negligently) by hypothetically substituting, for A's negligent shot, his taking proper care in shooting. We ask whether in that event C would have lost his eye from that set of con-

37. Toepel, above n.20, at pp.66, 72–5.
38. See, above, nn.8–15 and accompanying text.

ditions. If not, A's negligent shooting was a cause of C's loss of eyesight. But suppose that careful investigation shows that A's shot missed. In that case A's shot was not causally relevant to the outcome and we must construct another set of conditions, including B's shot, and test whether B's shot was a necessary member of that set of conditions which together produced the loss of eyesight. Toepel objects that this procedure involves deciding that A's shot was causally relevant before we test it for causal relevance.[39] That is not so. All we have decided before testing A's shot for relevance while provisionally omitting B's is that, as we know some of the INUS conditions for loss of eyesight, A's shot may on this occasion have been a causally relevant condition even in the absence of B's shot. It is true that the testing procedure is possible only if we know some causal regularities before we start. But we need not assume from the start that the outcome of the test will be positive.

A similar causal over-determination analysis may be applied to other cases in which two similar processes appear responsible for an event, for example, where two fires merge and jointly culminate in harm[40] or where the pollution created by a number of persons independently pollutes a stream or lake.[41]

B. Over-determination: Different Causal Processes

In other over-determination cases the two sets of conditions involve qualitatively different causal processes, such as poisoning and dehydration, the various stages of which have been studied and can be distinguished. In that case, if we know enough about the stages by which the events came about we can generally tell, even in cases of over-determination, which causal process ran its course and which was frustrated. So in the case of the desert traveller[42] – where A poisons C's water keg, B empties the keg before C drinks the poisoned water, and C dies of thirst – it now seems to me that B causes C's death. I

39. Toepel, above n.20, at p.69.
40. Wright, *Pruning*, above n.2, at pp.1018, 1022.
41. See generally *id.* p.1035–7.
42. James A. McLaughlin, "Proximate Cause", 39 *Harv. Law Rev.* 149, 155 n.25 (1925–1926); Hart and Honoré, *Causation* (2nd ed.), above n.7, at pp.239–41; Mackie, above n.2, at pp.44–6.

regret that, despite criticism by Mackie,[43] since endorsed by Wright,[44] the second edition of Hart and Honoré resisted this conclusion.[45] My current reasoning is that B's conduct introduces a condition, lack of water, that in the circumstances, including the absence of an alternative water supply, is sufficient to bring about and does bring about C's death from dehydration.

It is also true that B saved C from dying of poison. But this is not relevant in an explanatory inquiry, since B's act adequately explains how C's death came about (through dehydration), nor should it be relevant in a wrongful death action or prosecution for homicide. If B, not realizing that the water keg was poisoned, emptied it intending to harm C or negligently failing in his duty to C, the deceased's widow ought therefore to succeed in a wrongful death action[46] – though since C was doomed in any event the damages will be minimal. On the other hand if B realized that the water was poisoned and emptied the keg to prevent C drinking the poisoned water, and supposing that an alternative supply could be found in time to save C, B would still unintentionally have "caused" C's death; but he would not be legally responsible for doing so. There is no need to postulate any special legal concept of cause in order to understand this type of case.

In cases of over-determination, where different causal processes are associated with the two conditions that are causal candidates, there should be no need to show that one of them was a NESS condition of death *as and how the death occurred* (e.g. by dehydration on Tuesday rather than by poisoning on Monday).[47] That would be to require establishing the very point in issue, namely how the victim's death came about. What has to be shown in a tort action is that the defendant's wrongful act caused the harm, in this case the victim's death. We know from the way in which the law structures actions for wrongful death that what is legally relevant is death, not death at this or that time or place or by this or that process.[48] However, the plaintiff (the widow) has to identify the death for which she claims redress.

43. Mackie, above n.2, at pp.44, 46–7.
44. Wright, *Pruning*, above n.1, at p.1024.
45. Hart and Honoré, *Causation*, above n.5, at pp.219–20; (2nd ed.), above n.7, at pp.239–41. See Mackie, above n.2, at pp.45–6.
46. And, if the harm was intentional, B will be guilty of homicide.
47. As suggested by Mackie, above n.2, at p.46; Toepel, above n.20, at pp.70, 78–9.
48. Wright, *Causation*, above n.17, at pp.1777–8; Wright, *Pruning*, above n.2, at pp.1025–6; Puppe, *Der Erfolg*, above n.19, at pp.863, 867–8.

This requires that the victim, place and time be specified. She has also to show that the defendant's wrongful act *caused* the death, which involves showing that some causal process initiated by the defendant brought it about. In the water keg example, that B's conduct (in emptying the water keg) was a condition of C's death by dehydration is relevant because the process of dehydration connects B's act by a series of stages with C's death. To establish that this process occurred is relevant because, given the plurality of possible causes of death, it is necessary for C's widow to point to a specific causal process that links the two, and dehydration is such a process.

C. Over-determination: Harm that Has Already Occurred

Although philosophers may debate the possibility of backward causation, it seems clear that it is impossible to cause an event that has already occurred. One can flog a dead horse but not kill it. On the other hand one can kill someone who has only a moment to live, as in the case where defendants were alleged to have negligently electrocuted the deceased boy as he fell to certain death.[49] The fact that our concept of cause does not allow for causing harm that has already occurred can give rise to a problem of over-determination when the harm consists of depriving someone of future opportunities.

Suppose that A negligently injures C, a wrestler, so that he is permanently disabled from wrestling. Six months later B independently and negligently runs C over so that, even had he not been injured the first time, he would not have been able to wrestle in future. That B's act was independent implies that the first injury did not contribute to the second, for example by preventing C from avoiding the second accident.[50]

What is the status of C's claim to loss of future earnings as a wrestler? A, and only A, is clearly responsible for what C would have earned in the six months following the first injury. As regards C's lost wrestling earnings following the second injury, however, responsibility is much less clear. B will plead that he did not cause C's disability as a wrestler even in part since C was permanently disabled already.

49. *Dillon* v. *Twin State Gas & Elec. Co.*, 163 Atl. 111 (1932).
50. The facts are suggested by *Baker* v. *Willoughby* [1970] AC 467. Cf. *Jobling* v. *Associated Dairies*, [1982] AC 794.

Yet A will plead that his liability is limited to the six months' earnings alone, since, as it turns out, C would not have been able to wrestle for more than that period in any event. If both of these arguments are accepted, C, having been wrongfully injured on two occasions, obtains less than had he been injured only once, which is unsatisfactory. Yet this is not like the case of simultaneous over-determination where each agent can properly be said to have caused the same injury. Someone who claims to have lost future opportunities of earning money must show that he would have been able to take advantage of those opportunities in the absence of the wrongful act of which he complains. For example, if after six months C had died of a heart attack, not brought on by the injury inflicted by A, his estate could not claim loss of earnings for the period after he was dead. A dead man cannot wrestle, and there is no reason to impose on A the risk that C could die of natural causes unconnected with A's wrongful act.

There are two possible ways round the difficulty, one of which is consistent with causal principles while the other rests on a basis of risk-allocation. The first solution is to hold that there is a cause of action in tort law for depriving someone by a wrongful act of a tort remedy that would otherwise have been available to him. In the injured wrestler case, B has deprived C of a tort remedy against A for his lost wrestling earnings following the second injury. This cause of action, if it existed, would be like the suggested remedy, now much discussed, against a defendant who wrongfully deprives a plaintiff of a chance.[51] The alternative way of solving the injured wrestler conundrum is to treat is to treat A as guaranteeing C that he will not be deprived of his prospective remedy for loss of earnings by a later wrongful act of someone else. To construct such a guarantee is to provide a non-causal basis of liability, an example of the familiar principle by which the risk of harm to C is sometimes placed on A. Here the risk would be imposed on A as a result of A's wrongdoing, just as in the law of sale risk is sometimes transferred to the seller because of his failure to deliver goods on time. The justification for putting the risk on A would be that it is the function of the law to protect people against wrongful invasions of their rights. Rather than let a person

51. Wright, *Pruning*, above n.2, at pp.1067–72. A "lost chance" case may arise, for example, if a doctor negligently fails to diagnose a progressive disease such as cancer in a timely manner, and so deprives the patient of, say, a twenty per cent chance of recovery. Causes of action along these lines, whatever their intrinsic merits, do no violence to causal principles.

who has suffered two wrongs go without remedy, it is better to make the first wrongdoer guarantee him against the economic consequences of a later tort by some third person. To do this would not be to introduce a special legal sense of cause. It would be to substitute, for liability based on causing harm, liability based on risk-allocation.

D. Indeterminacy

Indeterminacy presents a difficulty for the NESS theory. If the world is indeterminate, we cannot assemble a set of conditions invariably sufficient to produce a given outcome. The outcome may usually follow, but there will be occasions when it does not. At most there may be a certain probability that on a given occasion the outcome will follow. An indeterminate world also presents a difficulty for the but-for theory, since in an indeterminate world we cannot accurately calculate what would have happened in the absence of a particular wrongful act. But, if it is permissible with Mackie to fall back on our intuitive grasp of but-for relationships,[52] the difficulty is less serious for the but-for than for the NESS theory.

Mackie, though leaving open whether the world really is indeterminate, argues that what we would say about causation in an indeterminate world supports the but-for theory.[53] He imagines two candy machines, both "indeterministic".[54] One never produces candy unless the proper coin is inserted, but does not always produce candy when it is. The other always produces candy when a coin is inserted, but sometimes does so without a coin. Applying the but-for test, Mackie thinks that we would say of the first machine that it caused the candy to appear when it did appear, but deny this for the second machine.

Mackie's argument is not convincing.[55] If we thought that the candy machine world was indeterminate we would have no reason to suppose that the first machine would not in future behave like the

52. See, above, text accompanying n.15.
53. Toepel, above n.20, at pp.61, 90–5.
54. Mackie, above n.2, at pp.40–3, 47.
55. Hart and Honoré (2nd ed.), above n.7, at pp.xl–xli, 235 n.56; Wright, *Pruning*, above n.2, at p.1029; Wright, *Causation*, above n.17, at pp.1777–8; cf. Toepel, above n.20, at pp.92–3.

second machine and produce candy without a coin being inserted, and vice versa for the second machine. We would have no reason to hold that the insertion of the coin caused the candy to appear in the one machine but not in the other. But, though their operation may be erratic, we believe that candy machines are deterministic.[56] We explain their deviant behaviour on the basis that, if the machine does not produce candy when a coin is inserted or does produce it when a coin is not inserted, the mechanism is faulty. In the first case, a counteracting factor is present; something in the machine has jammed and prevents the candy from emerging. Recall that in most sets of jointly sufficient conditions, one condition is the absence of counteracting conditions.[57] In the second case, given the plurality of causes, we conclude that an alternative set of INUS conditions for the production of candy is present, which might consist for example not in inserting a coin but in giving the machine a hefty kick when the mechanism is jammed.

The argument from an imagined indeterminate world does not support the but-for theory. What of the argument that the world really *is* indeterminate? The micro-level indeterminacy associated with quantum mechanics is not in point. As Wright neatly observes, it might be an obstacle to actions between fundamental particles, but it does not affect the macro-phenomena which are the law's concern. More baffling is the difficulty of tracing causal connection, or something like it, with human actions done for reasons – when one person provides another with a reason for doing so-and-so.[58] Although we have up to now discussed physical sequences of events as if they took place untroubled by human intervention, there are in practice few situations in tort law where a physical sequence of events is not partly determined by human decisions taken in the light of a situation as it develops. To take an example, adapted from Mackie,[59] suppose the question is whether Alec's statement caused Bill to hit Charles. If Alec said, for instance, that Charles was having an affair

56. Wright, *Pruning*, above n.1, at p.1029.

57. See above, nn.11–12 and accompanying text.

58. Hart and Honoré, *Causation* (2nd ed.), above n.7, at pp.51–61. For want of space I do not deal in this paper with the provision of opportunities which another person exploits or the furnishing of help of which another takes advantage. These are important legally and in ordinary life but are still more remote from physical sequences than is acting on a reason provided by another.

59. Mackie, above n.2, at p.43.

with Bill's girl-friend, it would be intelligible that what he said caused Bill to hit Charles. If one objects to the use of "caused" in a context where Bill should have controlled himself, other expressions such as "led", "induced", and "provoked" could replace it. The situation is of a type that often arises in tort law, for example in connection with false statements that induce others to invest money or persuasions that lead contracting parties to break their contracts. How should sequences of this sort, which involve providing reasons on which others act, be analysed?

It seems impossible to suppose a set of NESS conditions that would together be sufficient to produce Bill's assault on Charles. Many people believe that human conduct is not strictly determined. If so, one cannot even in principle assemble a set of conditions sufficient to induce a person to act in a particular way. Even if human action is determined, it will still not be possible to assemble a set of conditions of this sort. This is not merely because the reactions of human beings vary. A greater difficulty is that a person who has been confronted with a similar set of conditions in the past may, in the light of that experience, react differently on this occasion. It does not follow from Bill's reaction on this occasion that he would react similarly if told the same thing again. It does not follow that David would react in the same way if Alec told him the same thing about his (David's) girl-friend. Even with a great deal of information about people's characters and background, their reactions simply are not totally predictable. Moreover, any prediction, if known by the person about whom it is made, may provide a reason for reacting differently.

Thus, determinism in regard to human conduct, even if true, cannot be tested. Yet Bill's reaction is *explained* by what Alec said to him, and to that extent functions as a causal (or quasi-causal) explanation. What Alec said was in some sense sufficient in the circumstances to lead Bill to react as he did. Yet if we are to speak either of "causing" people to act or, more modestly, of influencing them in their decisions, a different account of the connection is called for.

Mackie thinks that our attitude to interpersonal transactions favours the but-for theory.[60] Had Alec not said what he did, we may be sure that Bill would not have hit Charles. But how can we tell this? Presumably because we have assembled, from our experience and that

60. Mackie, above n.2, at pp.121–6.

of others, not sets of INUS conditions relating to human behaviour, but some loose generalizations that tell us what sorts of reason people act on. In the present case the only reason that could explain Bill's attack was what Alec said to him. If Bill admits that this was why he struck Charles, the diagnosis is confirmed.

But this is not enough to show that the but-for theory explains the sort of connection involved in acting for a reason. For a person often has two or more (typically many more) reasons for reaching a decision and acting on it. A potential investor may be influenced by a false statement in a prospectus and by advice from his stockbroker. Suppose that for these two reasons he makes an ill-fated investment in Eldorado Mines. Nothing turns, it seems to me, on whether each reason was necessary or sufficient to persuade him to invest, or to dissuade him from changing his mind.[61] Would we conclude that the false statement did not induce him to make the investment if the advice from the stockbroker was also sufficient to persuade him to do so? If the investor is prepared to say truthfully that each of the reasons influenced him, it seems immaterial whether he is prepared to say that, but for one of them, he would not have reached the decision he did. The reasons on which he acts are precisely that – the reasons that, either individually or jointly, appeared to him sufficient and motivated him to decide and act.

Sam is offered a post in Middletown at an increased salary. Middletown is his wife's home town and she wishes to return there. Both of these factors – the increased salary and his wife's wishes – may be reasons sufficient to induce Sam to accept the offer, in which case neither is a but-for reason. Or both may be necessary elements in a set of reasons together sufficient to persuade Sam to accept the offer. In either case, Sam acts on those two reasons, which are either singly or jointly sufficient to persuade him. But along with these *reasons* that induce him to go to Middletown, there will be other *conditions* such that, had they not existed, he would have refused the offer. There are good schools in Middletown for the children; Middletown has a lively choral society. Had there not been good schools and a lively choral society Sam would have refused the offer; but they were not his

61. See *Australian Steel & Mining Corp.* v. *Corben* 1974 2 N.S.W.L.R. 202, 209; Hart and Honoré, *Causation* (2nd ed.), above n.7, at p.193. Compare, for criminal law, judgement of Feb. 24, 1959, BGH Gr. Sen. St., 13 Entscheidungen des Bundesgerichtshofes in Strafsachen [BGHSt] 15 (F.R.G.); contra Toepel, above n.20, at p.93.

reasons for accepting. So far as these reasons are concerned he might just as well have stayed where he was. But-for reasons are often not reasons for taking a decision or acting on it, but reasons against not taking it. They do not cause, lead, induce or prompt Sam to move, any more than the existence of the capitalist system induces the investor to put his money in Eldorado Mines.

It seems to me that we reach our conclusions about what caused, induced, persuaded, or provoked someone to act as he did in a way somewhat like but not identical with the way in which we reach conclusions about the causes of physical events. We cannot construct INUS conditions and NESS conditions for situations in which human beings make and act on decisions. But we know enough about the sorts of reason that motivate us to be able often to conclude that certain factors were singly or together sufficient for the decision. All that is meant by "sufficient" in this context is that they provide an adequate explanation of the decision, and that the person who takes the decision would acknowledge, if truthful, that these were his reasons. They were sufficient for this individual in this situation, though there is no implication that they would be sufficient for him or anyone else in a similar situation on another occasion. What we mean when we speak of "inducing", "persuading" etc. is to refer to reasons that seemed adequate to this person on this occasion and on which he therefore acted. Some or all of them may also have been necessary to the decision; and it is often a good procedure heuristically to ask whether the same decision would have been reached in the absence of a given reason. But the answer to this question is not decisive of the existence of a causal or quasi-causal relation between reason and action. It is no part of the meaning of "cause", "induce" etc. in interpersonal transactions that the person concerned would not have acted as he did, apart from the conduct of the person who is said to have induced him to act. The meaning of causal or quasi-causal connection is here closer to sufficiency that to necessity, but sufficiency not in the sense in which that term is used in regard to physical sequences, but rather in the sense of what someone regards as an adequate ground on which to decide and act in the circumstances.

4. Conclusion

Why is causation important in tort law? One reason is that to insist on causal connection between conduct and harm ensures that in general we impose liability only on those who, by intervening in the world, have changed the course of events for the worse. But what is it to change the course of events for the worse? Is it to do (1) something such that in the conditions prevailing harm comes about, or (2) something in the absence of which harm would not have come about? The first interpretation is that of the NESS theory (for physical sequences); and a variant of that theory can be used to explain what it is to influence human decisions and actions. The second interpretation is that of the but-for theory.

The first interpretation is to be preferred. Causing a given harmful result means, in relation to physical events, completing a set of conditions sufficient to bring it about, i.e. providing a NESS condition of that harm. In relation to influencing human action, it means providing a reason that the human agent accepts, often along with other reasons, as sufficient to induce him to decide and act as he does (to his or someone else's detriment).

On the other hand the but-for theory, though a useful heuristic device, provides the intuitively wrong answer in certain areas of overdetermination and indeterminacy. The explanation for this seems to be that our concept of cause derives ultimately from our search for recipes to bring about the outcomes we want. We look for sets of conditions that are sufficient (or, in the case of human decisions, that may be regarded by the agent as sufficient) to bring about a certain outcome. Knowledge of these sets of conditions, though nearly always imperfect, has many applications. In particular, it often enables us to explain puzzling events and, in many contexts of law, including tort law, to fix the outer limits of social responsibility for conduct.

That does not make the concept of cause a normative one. The same concept of cause is used for discovering recipes, for explaining events, and for assigning responsibility for outcomes. The normative elements are supplied by substantive tort law, which define the conduct that entails or may entail tort liability, and prescribes when causal connection between conduct and harm must be proved.

6

BEING RESPONSIBLE AND BEING A VICTIM OF CIRCUMSTANCE[1]

It is an honour to give the Maccabaean lecture in Jurisprudence, and to celebrate Cromwell's decision, taken in 1655 on sound legal advice, to allow the return of the Jews to England, the more so in view of my personal debt to a great Jewish lawyer and philosopher, Herbert Hart. The Maccabaean lecturer ought in decency to address, at a theoretical level, some puzzle that worries philosophers, lawyers and ordinary people. In what follows I wrestle with a problem of this sort: the relation between treating people as responsible and treating them as victims of their circumstances.

It may be helpful at the outset to outline the argument that follows. I take a wide view of what it is to be responsible, while conceding that the term is often used more narrowly. We can be responsible even when we are not morally to blame or legally liable for our actions. We can be responsible for unintended aspects or outcomes of our conduct and for actions performed when we are not fully capable of acting rationally or when our freedom is restricted. Moreover, this wide conception of responsibility is to be welcomed and defended against attempts to undermine it. Moral blame and legal liability, especially criminal liability, are narrower notions. When they are present their force is or should be mitigated when the person in question, though responsible, was not fully capable of acting rationally or their freedom to choose was distorted by their circumstances. To that extent we can properly treat people both as responsible and as victims of circumstance.

1. The Maccabaean lecture in Jurisprudence for 1997, delivered on 17 February 1998 and published in *Proceedings of the British Academy* vol. 97 (1998) pp.169–87. Copyright The British Academy 1998. I am grateful to Andrew Ashworth, Tom Bingham, Edwin Cameron, Jean Floud, Roger Hood, John Gardner, Tom Nagel, Joseph Raz, Stephen Shute and, not least, Bernard Williams, all of whom read a draft of this lecture and, without prejudice, gave me the benefit of their advice.

So much by way of introduction. Of the various ways of looking at human conduct, two seem at first sight difficult, if not impossible, to reconcile. We think of human behaviour as something for which, except in rare cases, the person whose conduct is in question – the agent, to use a convenient term – is responsible.[2] Agents are responsible because the behaviour is theirs. They have intervened in the world and changed it. Their conduct is the cause of that change.

At times, however, we think of human conduct differently: as the outcome of factors that cause and so explain it. These include genetic make-up, environment, temperament, and the pressures to which we are all subject. Let us call them "circumstances", and note that in this sense circumstances include internal factors (how one is constituted) as well as external ones, past and present. Circumstances can be seen as responsible, or partly responsible, for what we do. We are, up to a point, trapped by them. But they are responsible only in a weak sense. People can be called to account, but these background factors cannot be. So, when circumstances are said to be responsible for behaviour, the word is used in the sense in which any cause is responsible for its consequences – the short-circuit is responsible for the fire it brings about.

These different ways of looking at conduct are familiar outside the law. They also feature within it, specially in criminal law and procedure. In general criminal law treats adults as responsible and so liable to sanctions for the offences they commit. But sometimes it holds that they are not criminally liable, are guilty of a lesser offence, or should be punished less severely than normal offenders. One ground for this – not the only one[3] – is that, when they acted, they were not (or not fully) in a position to reach a rational decision. By a rational decision is meant one that relates the conduct to the agent's general aims, though it may not conform to law or social mores. Those who are not capable of a deciding rationally in this sense are regarded as not to blame, or as less to blame than they would otherwise have been.

Why capacity and blame should be related in this way is not at first sight obvious: I shall return to the puzzle later on. But the link is a

2. The term "agent" is used because our concern will be more with positive action than with failure to act, though this will be touched on briefly.
3. I leave on one side for the moment social and moral deprivation, but return to it at the

powerful one, and it fits the retributive notion that punishment should not be disproportionate to blame.[4] In English law the link between capacity, blame and punishment underlies several features of the criminal process: the defence of insanity, the law relating to "abnormality of mind" (resulting in "diminished responsibility"),[5] the treatment of infanticide as less serious than murder,[6] and many matters that are routinely put forward in mitigation (that the offence was conduced to by domestic tension, emotional stress, financial pressures, addiction to alcohol or drugs).[7] These factors are stressed both in pleas in mitigation and in the pre-sentence reports that are available to judges and presumably influence them in sentencing. They are thought to impair rational judgement and to affect self-control and other aspects of rationality such as cognition. Short-term factors can also be seen as affecting a person's capacity for self-control. Provocation in the form of physical aggression or grossly insulting behaviour can reduce liability from murder to manslaughter if it results in a temporary loss of self-control, and otherwise may be a mitigating factor that affects the sentence imposed. In all these cases, the agent's ability to behave sensibly is taken to be impaired. The agent is in a broad sense responsible, since the conduct is in some respects intentional and so, at least in our culture, invites approval or criticism. But criminal liability is excluded or its impact reduced.

The incidents of the criminal process mentioned enter the law at different points and have different effects. The law is reluctant to accept impaired capacity as a complete defence to a criminal charge; it is much readier to treat it as relevant to sentencing. Yet they are all instances of "responsible but . . ." and it makes for clarity to think of

---

4. A.J. Ashworth, *Sentencing and Criminal Justice* (2nd ed. 1995) [hereafter *Sentencing*] ch.4 (proportionality). Several other notions – deterrence, incapacitation, stigmatization – enter into the rationale of punishment but I concentrate in this lecture on retribution, which is certainly one element in it.
5. Homicide Act 1957 s.2.
6. Infanticide Act 1938 s.1(1).
7. Many other matters can be relied on in mitigation, such as the offender's youth, contrition and co-operation with the authorities e.g. by pleading guilty: Ashworth, *Sentencing*, pp.133–49; Halsbury's *Laws of England* 11.2 paras. 1189–91; D.A. Thomas, *Principles of Sentencing* (2nd ed. 1979) pp.194–222. Sometimes it is not clear (illness, homelessness, unemployment) whether the factors relied on are meant to account for the offence or to show that the offender is so disadvantaged already that punishment will merely add to existing handicap. I am concerned here with those factors that have a bearing on the convicted person's deciding to act as they did, on which see J. Shapland, *Between Conviction and Sentence. The Process of Mitigation* (1981).

them as cases in which the agent is responsible but not, or not fully, to blame. If responsibility and capacity-linked-to-blame are treated as separate in this way,[8] the term "diminished responsibility" can be seen as a shorthand way of referring to cases where an agent is responsible but not wholly to blame. There are no degrees of responsibility, but rather degrees of capacity to control one's behaviour. If so, a person who is in a broad sense responsible for conduct may be more or less exposed to criminal liability or moral censure on that account.

Though the examples given come from English law, there are parallels in most, perhaps all, other systems. Nor is there anything peculiar to the law about viewing human conduct in the light of the agent's capacity for self-control and rational decision. In everyday life similar factors are thought to exclude or reduce blame for the bad things that people do to others and to themselves.[9]

An awkward question then presents itself. How can people both be responsible for what they do and at the same time be caused to act as they do by circumstances that impair their self-control? Must we, to be consistent, choose between these perspectives? If we can properly combine them, as in practice we do in ordinary life and in the law, when is it appropriate to look on people as victims of circumstance?

I think we may properly combine these ways of assessing our own and other people's conduct. But how far it is wise to do so depends on how far we think it desirable to press the search for the causes of and remedies for things that go wrong in our society. "The choice of stance is up to us".[10] An example will show what is meant. When someone has been disabled in a road accident it is proper, depending on the context, to pick out as the cause of their disability the medical condition that affects them, the accident that caused the medical condition, the driver's misjudgement, the disrepair of the road that

8. For the argument that responsibility, unlike blame, need not depend on choices being open see B. Williams, *Making Sense of Humanity* [hereafter *Humanity*] pp.17–19.

9. On the comparison between mitigation in court and the judgements we make in everyday life see Shapland, above n.7, ch.3.

10. D.M. Mackay, "The Use of Behavioural Language to Refer to Mechanical Processes", *Brit. Jour. Phil. Sci.* (1962) 89–103. I agree with D.C. Dennett, "Mechanism and Responsibility" [hereafter *Mechanism*], in *Essays on Freedom of Action* (ed. T. Honderich 1973) pp.159–74 that the choice of stance (e.g. intentional rather than physical) should not be endowed with a premature moral dimension. The initial question is whether we regard agents as people, not how we judge them morally or legally.

brought about the accident, or the shortage of funds that led to the road's disrepair. Any of these can properly be cited as the cause of the victim's disability. No error of fact or logic is committed in selecting one rather than the other. The choice between them depends on the aim of the inquiry. Is its focus medical science, an insurance policy covering accidental injury, a lawsuit for negligence, a study of road safety, or an investigation of local authority finance? What is picked out as the cause depends on how far back, and for what purpose, we want to trace the causal process.

In much the same way, surely, people can in principle be both responsible agents and the victims of circumstance. They can be both the authors of the good or harm that their actions bring about and be caused to act as they do. The question is not which view is exclusively correct but which is preferable when we assess people's behaviour in everyday life and the law. The answer must be that in general we do well, indeed we are impelled (for reasons that I hope to make clear), to treat ourselves and others as responsible agents. But the argument for welcoming this conclusion is not that our behaviour is uncaused – something that we cannot know and which, if true, would be a surprise – but that to treat people as responsible promotes individual and social well-being. It does this in two ways. It helps to preserve social order by encouraging good and discouraging bad behaviour. At the same time, it makes possible a sense of personal character and identity that is valuable for its own sake. But there is a proper place, which it is important to try to define, for the "victim of circumstance" perspective.

1. Responsibility

To see how this can be the case, it helps to turn to the notion of responsibility,[11] which, as mentioned, is taken in a broad sense and does not necessarily import legal liability or moral blame, though it is a condition of both.

11. H.L.A. Hart "Varieties of Responsibility", 83 *Law Quarterly Review* (1967) [hereafter *Varieties*] 363–4 argued that the primary sense of responsibility was that of answering a charge. I am not sure about this, but in any case the underlying idea is embodied in the Greek *aitios*, being the cause of something (B. Williams, *Shame and Necessity*, 1993, [hereafter *Shame*] pp.52–4), with the corollary of having to answer for it, not necessarily before a court. This combination yields the notion of responsibility for one's own (in some aspect intentional) conduct. This notion is in turn

There are three sources of human responsibility. The primary one is our responsibility for our own conduct. Then there is the responsibility for other people, things[12] and events[13] that we choose to take on. Lastly, there is the responsibility that society thrusts on us, either informally or through the law, for example responsibility to one's family and community.

If these three sources are kept in mind, some false ideas can be nailed at the outset. One is that we are responsible only for our own behaviour; a second that we are responsible only when we are to blame; a third that we are responsible only when we choose to be. None of these is true. Being responsible for our own behaviour is the primary example of responsibility but not the only one. A person can be both responsible and legally liable for something they have not done. An employer can, for example, be vicariously liable for the act of an employee. Nor is this a legal quirk. People can be morally responsible for the behaviour of others.[14] Parents can, for example, be morally responsible for the way in which their children behave even when they are not legally liable for it. In that case the person who is morally responsible should act somewhat as if the responsibility were legal. If the children have broken the neighbour's window they should pay for the damage. This is one of the many ways in which morality, as conceived in western culture, follows the legal model.

---

capable of extension by analogy to the second and third sources of responsibility mentioned in the text, where these elements are not necessarily all present, for example because the person responsible has to answer for the conduct of some other person of which he or she is not the cause.

12. D.C. Dennett, *Elbow Room* (1984) p.85: "I *take* responsibility for any thing I make and then inflict upon the general public". It is not in fact necessary to have made it. The seller of something manufactured by another is responsible for inflicting it on the public.
13. This may seem surprising, but insurers typically make themselves responsible for paying for losses caused by events such as shipwrecks.
14. "Morality" here refers to that type of ethical thought according to which behaviour should be guided by something analogous to law (J. Feinberg, *Doing and Deserving*, 1984, pp.30–7) in that moral reasoning issues in practical conclusions in the form of obligations. See B. Williams in *World, Mind and Ethics. Essays on the Ethical Philosophy of Bernard Williams* (ed. J.E.J. Altham and R. Harrison 1995) p.204. Morality in this sense is alien to Greek thought, since classical Greece had no lawyers (i.e. to whom law was a distinct intellectual discipline), just as Rome had no (original) philosophers. Nietzsche, *On the Genealogy of Morals* (1887 trans. W. Kaufmann and R.J. Hollingdale 1967) p.64 put the point about the relation between legal and moral guilt, duty etc. in a typically provocative way.

As these examples show, we can be responsible for the behaviour of others without necessarily being to blame. The employer or parent is sometimes but not always to blame for the employee or child's behaviour. The same is true of our own behaviour. We can be responsible for what we do by sheer accident, like unavoidably tripping someone. The responsibility need not, of course, be legal, but in such a case, though not to blame, we incur a moral obligation. An apology is called for, and the person who has been tripped must be helped up and if necessary taken for treatment.

Thirdly, when people are responsible it is not always because they have chosen to be responsible. Sometimes they have not chosen to be responsible because they have not chosen to do the thing for which they are held responsible.[15] When they are responsible for their own doings this is usually because they have chosen to act as they did. But at times they have no real choice. Someone who is forced to hand over money by a mugger is responsible for handing it over. It may well have been the right thing to do, though the victim had no real option. And at times our convictions leave us with no real option. In such cases not only are we responsible for what we do but we want, like Luther, to be seen as responsible: "Here I stand. I can do no other".[16] But even those who choose to act as they do do not necessarily choose to be responsible for what they do. When they are morally or legally responsible for failing to act, failing, for example, to help a friend in need or to pay income tax, they may have chosen not to help or not to pay but they have not chosen to be responsible for the default. Social or legal norms required them to act. Their duty arose from friendship or membership of the community, and though they may have chosen to befriend someone or to belong to a certain community, they do not choose what friendship or citizenship requires.

Responsibility is not confined, then, either in law or morals, to responsibility for one's own conduct or for one's fault or for situations in which one has chosen to be responsible. It has a wider significance. That we should think of ourselves as responsible agents, as taking on responsibility for other people and things, and as having it thrust on us, is what makes possible a shared sense of one's identity and character and of that of others. It makes possible a life in common in which

---

15. Williams, *Humanity*, above n.8, at p.4.
16. Words attributed to Luther at Worms in 1521: *Hier stehe ich. Ich kann nicht anders. Gott helfe mich.*

people relate to one another as individuals, each with distinctive traits, virtues and shortcomings, and with a history that is largely made up of what they have done, of their achievements and failures.[17]

To grasp what is involved in being responsible, a good start is to consider the ways in which we take on responsibility.[18] Most of them involve assuming control of some situation or purporting to control it. The manager of a business, the leader of a political party, the head of a school takes on a role by virtue of which they are responsible for the business, the party or the school. If it does well they gain credit and are commended for its success; if badly, they incur discredit and may be censured for its shortcomings. People also take on transient responsibilities, divorced from any sustained role, say for arranging a meeting or seeing that a friend's children get to school on time. When they promise that something is the case, for example that the car they are lending is in good condition, they make themselves responsible for its condition. If the children get to school on time, if the car is sound, they gain credit; if not, they incur discredit.

The credit or discredit that comes from taking on responsibilities need not have legal implications. The business manager may not be legally liable for the losses the business incurs. The party leader is not legally liable for the party's failure to be re-elected. Nor need the credit or blame be moral. Though moral virtue may help to ensure success, success may also be due, or partly due, to natural ability or luck – by which I mean events that are unforeseen and often unforeseeable.[19] The market moves in the business manager's favour, the political opposition is bankrupt. The manager or leader then gets credit for success, but not moral credit. The same is true of failure,

17. "A conception of personal identity according to which each of us is . . . a being essentially related to others by ties of recognition and concern": M. Nussbaum, "Aristotle, nature and ethics", in *World, Mind and Ethics*, above n.14, at p.109. The theme was developed, and acquired the label "outcome responsibility" in H.L.A. Hart and T. Honoré, *Causation in the Law* (2nd ed. 1985) [hereafter *Causation*] intro. lxxx–lxxxi. See also chs.2 and 4 above.

18. Something wider than taking on a role, on which see Hart, *Varieties*, above n.11, at pp.347–8. One can take on responsibility, for example, for the truth of some assertion.

19. This refers to luck as to the circumstances in which we find ourselves and to how our actions turn out. There can also be good and bad luck in the way in which we are constituted, our inclinations, capacities and temperament: T. Nagel, *Mortal Questions*, (1979) pp.28, 32–3. Though for some people "luck averages out in the long run" (Dennett, *Elbow Room*, above n.12, at p.95) it can have an unexpected and unwelcome impact on a particular action for which the agent is responsible.

which can come about through moral failings, but also from want of skill or bad luck, or a combination of these. In this connection the word "blame" can be misleading. Some forms of blame carry no moral or legal baggage. People are blamed for actions that exhibit want of skill, bad judgement and inattention: a footballer for not scoring when he had an open goal, a politician for advocating a policy that lost votes, a motorist for overlooking a convenient short cut.

Much the same is true when, instead of people taking on responsibility, society thrusts it on them by requiring them to do something. Here also they gain credit for fulfilling the obligations they owe to their family and friends and to the community, and discredit if they fail to fulfil them. The credit is often slight, even minimal, but requirements like that of compulsory military service can lead to one's being ordered to the battle front. Duty may then require something close to heroism.

Societies and individuals could not have devised these ways of taking on responsibility or of thrusting it on others unless they first understood what it was for people to be responsible for their actions.[20] This primary responsibility, unlike responsibility for what people take on, attaches automatically and with the feature already noted, that they gain credit for getting things right, but incur blame for getting them wrong.

Our responsibility for what we do is connected with the control we have over our conduct. But, though our conduct must have an intentional aspect, what we do includes its unintended aspects[21] and consequences.[22] If Oedipus (intentionally) kills a man in a quarrel and that man turns out to be his father, he has killed his father. If while driving (intentionally) I accidentally run someone over, and the injured person dies as a result, I have killed that person. Though in the main we control our conduct, to succeed in what we set out to do

20. Including responsibility for their actions in taking on responsibilities for other people and events.
21. Williams, *Shame*, above n.11, at p.69 (Oedipus).
22. This is to adopt the idea of action as an intervention in the world which is in some aspect intentional. The limit of our intervention is set by later interventions, so that the consequences that form part of our action do not extend indefinitely. The theme is developed in Hart and Honoré, *Causation*, above n.17, at pp.68–81 and Honoré, "Causation and Remoteness of Damage", *International Encyclopedia of Comparative Law* 11 (1971) ch.7. For a more restricted view of action in the context of criminal law see Maurach/Zipf, *Strafrecht* (6th ed.) Allg. Teil I (1983) 198–96.

depends partly on other people and on luck.[23] To act is to some extent to take a chance,[24] to mortgage one's credit,[25] since we decide what to do in conditions of incomplete certainty. Moreover, the difference in this respect between being responsible for what we do ourselves and taking on responsibility for other people or things is a matter of degree. A competent motorist setting out from Oxford to Glasgow will probably arrive safely. Still, something turns on the road conditions, the reactions of other drivers, and sheer luck.[26] When we act we intervene in the world, and, since unlike the objects of scientific experiment, we are not insulated from our environment, to act is to interact with other people and things. Inevitably there is some risk that what we decide to do will go wrong. It is no accident that a person who is risk-averse tends to be inactive.

Responsibility, then, whether it attaches automatically or is voluntarily taken on or is imposed by society, involves a combination of actual or assumed control and risk. To be responsible is to take the credit and discredit arising from something that is in a sense ours, either because it is our conduct (and conduct invites self-assessment or assessment by others), or because we have made it ours by taking on responsibility for it or have had it thrust on us. "We" is to be understood broadly. Groups and organisations such as businesses and states can be responsible as well as individuals. But it is central to responsibility that it exposes the individual or group to risk. Some thinkers have indeed argued that criminal liability[27] and moral

23. T. Nagel, *Mortal Questions*, above n.19, at pp.25–6.
24. Because "how things turn out determines what [the agent] has done": Nagel, *Mortal Questions*, pp.29–30.
25. I developed this theme in "Responsibility and Luck. The Moral Basis of Strict Liability", 104 *Law Quarterly Review* (1988) 530–53, reprinted as essay 2. The argument is that when we act we bet on things turning out right, not only in the spectacular cases (such as Chamberlain signing the Munich agreement) where the agent knows in advance that he will be judged according to how things turn out, but in general. See also Dennett, *Elbow Room*, above n.12, at p.165 ("when people get caught in wrong deeds, their gambles wise or foolish have simply lost").
26. But careful foresight can reduce the role of luck in what a person does: Dennett, *Elbow Room* pp.92–9.
27. A.J. Ashworth, "Belief, Intent and Criminal Liability", in *Oxford Essays in Jurisprudence* (Third Series ed. J. Eekelaar and J. Bell 1987) pp.1–31; "Taking the Consequences", in *Action and Value in Criminal Law* (ed. S. Shute, J. Gardner and J. Horder 1993) pp.107–24, criticised by R.A. Duff, *Intention, Agency and Criminal Liability* (1990) ch.8; "Acting, Trying and Criminal Liability", in *Action and Value in Criminal Law*, pp.75–106.

blame[28] should never depend on luck. That is a possible, though in my view mistaken, view. But the issue it raises is not one about responsibility but about the consequences attaching to it. It may be that people, though responsible for doing harm, should not be made criminally liable or morally blamed for it unless they intended or foresaw the harm. But it does not follow that no one can be morally responsible as a result of bad luck. For that to be true we should have to adopt a narrowly effort-based view of human action, according to which what someone has done is identified with what they tried to do, and never constituted by its unintended outcome. Or we might opt for a selfish conception of morality, so that, for example, a relative could not be responsible for bringing up an orphaned child since the death of the child's parents was, from the relative's point of view, an unexpected piece of bad luck. It would be no part of that morality to fix people with responsibility for those who unexpectedly suffered misfortune. Spouses could not take one another for better or worse. Could there be such a morality? I am unsure, but, if there were, many would prefer not to be part of the society in which it prevailed.

Responsibility, then, involves taking risks. But why should we welcome the fact that we live in a society in which we are responsible for our conduct and take on or have thrust on us a wide range of responsibilities for people and things?[29] The prime reason can hardly be that the system of responsibility enables us to decide when people can be morally blamed for things that go wrong or when legal sanctions can be imposed on them. These are important but secondary aspects of the institution. They back up its primary function, which is to promote self-respect and individual and social well-being. Being responsible serves as an incentive to aim at and succeed in doing things that are regarded as valuable. In that way people gain credit for success in worthwhile activities (achievements) and avoid the discredit that attaches to failure in worthwhile activities (botches) and success in nefarious ones (misdeeds). If people were not responsible for what

28. B. Williams, "Moral Luck", *Proc. Aristotelian Soc. S.V.* 50 (1976); *Humanity*, above n.8, ch.21; T. Nagel "Moral Luck" in *Mortal Questions*, above n.19, ch.3.

29. Dennett, *Elbow Room*, above n.12, at pp.153–72 has a good discussion of why it is "rational for us to [esteem free will and] covet responsibility" (p.155) and why a well-designed society should provide for "some measure of arbitrariness and wise risk taking" (p.164). The value he attaches to free-will, as opposed to freedom, seems however misplaced (below n.39).

they did the movements involved would be those of their bodies, but the achievements, botches and misdeeds would not be theirs. They would not be actions, since actions have an intentional aspect, and there can be no intention without a person to do the intending.[30] Their behaviour would be the outcome of circumstances to which it would be pointless to attach credit or discredit.

Only by being responsible for what we do and take on can we be motivated to get things right.[31] But responsibility for our actions comes with a price tag. Not everything that is socially approved is morally admirable. Nonconformists and rebels have their value. The institution of being responsible works best when the motive of securing approval is combined, and if necessary overridden, by a willingness to take responsibility for unpopular, mistaken or wrong actions. Though the motive of seeking credit and avoiding discredit is essential to the working of responsibility, it does not follow that we are responsible only for those actions which, if successful, redound to our credit in the eyes of others. Other values that relate closely to our sense of identity, in particular self-respect and concern for autonomy, impel us to accept responsibility even for actions which seem to others (and perhaps in retrospect to ourselves), to be wrong. This is true even as regards those aspects and consequences of our conduct that we did not intend.

Though actions, as noted, must have an intentional aspect[32] – they must under some description have been intended – they commonly have unintended aspects as well. We do one thing meaning to do another, or meaning to do it but not foreseeing its outcome. It is then important to our sense of ourselves as persons to accept responsibility for what was not intended or foreseen. Consider the testimony of Vaclav Havel,[33] former dissident, now president of the Czech republic. When detained for the first time, he wrote and signed what he thought was a cleverly phrased letter to the Public Prosecutor asking

30. This remains true even if the notion of a person possessing in a self a "locus of self-control" (Dennett, *Elbow Room*, above n.12, at p.81) is in some sense a construct. It is a necessary construct if we are to embrace the intentional stance and the idea of responsibility.

31. Dennett, *Elbow Room*, above n.12, at p.165.

32. Perhaps there can be sub-intentional actions: B. O'Shaughnessy, *The Will. A Dual Aspect Theory* (1980) ch.10.

33. V. Havel, *Letters to Olga* (translated P. Wilson 1988) nos. 138, 139.

to be released from detention. In doing so he came, without meaning to, dangerously close to saying what the authorities wanted to hear. They released him and then exploited the letter to discredit him. It was only five years later, when detained again, that Havel stopped trying to explain away his mistake and came to accept full responsibility for what he had done. "The mistake lay", he puts it, "in an unconscious effort to localise the essential cause of my failure somewhere "outside" in "circumstances", "conditions", "external factors or influences". Redress lay in "assuming full responsibility here for one's elsewhere, today for one's own yesterday" so that "the 'I' achieves continuity and identity with the self".

The style of Havel's explanation is metaphysical, but the underlying idea is clear. Our identity and integrity depend on taking responsibility for the way in which we act or have acted in the past even in its unintended aspects.[34] The same is true by analogy of states. To accept responsibility for the unintended consequences of state action or default (e.g. the deaths in the Irish famine of 1845, the Armenian deportations of 1915 onwards, the concentration camps of the Boer War), can be for a nation the condition of self-respect and of reconciliation with the unintended victims of government action.

It may be objected that to treat people as responsible for what they do even in its unintended aspects is to ask too much of them. But to do so is not in itself to attach to them moral blame or legal sanction. It means basically that the person or group in question must accept what has happened as their doing and so open to assessment, favourable or unfavourable. If what happened was bad, they will have a moral obligation to do something to put it right, for example to acknowledge it and apologise, even though they were not morally to blame. That may be the whole extent of the obligation arising from their responsibility – which is not to underrate the importance of apologising when an apology is due.[35]

---

34. Cf. "The mature agent . . . will recognise his relation to his acts in their undeliberated, and also in their unforeseen and unintended aspects . . . he will be able to acknowledge more generally that he can be as responsible for some things that he did not intend much as he is for things that he did intend, and in ways that have nothing to do with the law of negligence": Williams, *Humanity*, above n.8, p.32 cf. *Shame*, above n.11, ch.3.
35. The importance of acknowledging that one has hurt someone, even though unintentionally, is captured in eastern Christianity by asking for forgiveness for sins "voluntary and involuntary".

Is even this too much to expect? Remember that we do not have the option of claiming responsibility when things turn out well and disclaiming it when they turn out badly. The principle involved is that of taking the rough with the smooth. More precisely, those who control a situation from which they may derive either benefit or detriment are entitled to the benefit that in the upshot accrues from it but must take the risk of any corresponding detriment. This principle has been developed mainly in legal contexts, such as sales, property transfers and vicarious liability. For that reason philosophers do not usually regard it, or at any rate mention it, as an aspect of justice. It looks, however, very like a species of distributive justice, since the distribution of burdens is the counterpart of the distribution of benefits.[36] But, however it is classified, its moral force can hardly be denied.[37]

Is it an objection to this wide view of responsibility that being responsible for one's conduct, with its concomitant credit and discredit, is in the interest only of those who attract more credit than discredit overall? And what of the inadequates, so prominent in the criminal process, who persistently go astray? What of the deviants who pursue anti-social aims? To draw up a balance sheet is a complicated matter. People cannot be sure in advance whether their activities are likely to yield a positive balance. And even those who incur more discredit than credit, gain protection against the harm that others might otherwise do them, from the fact that the others will be held responsible for their actions. Moreover, those who are inadequate or deviant should, and for the most part do, wish to be held responsible for their actions. They wish their autonomy to be affirmed rather than denied. Their sense of themselves as persons, even inadequate persons, is largely built up from their consciousness of what they have done. Their actions, though they reflect their background and make-up, progressively determine their character both in their own eyes and those of others. Being responsible for them is crucial to their sense of identity as persons who develop and change over time. If their behaviour could not be attributed to them in this way, they would have to conceive of themselves as attenuated beings:

36. Above pp.78–80.

37. Though we need not be morally to blame in order to be responsible the "taking the rough with the smooth" principle provides an argument in favour of our acknowledging responsibility for our actions.

objects to which things happen.[38] If they were not prepared to treat themselves as the authors of their conduct they could not even minimally aspire to dignity, pride or self-confidence. Since those who are inadequate or deviant need these attributes as much as, or more than, others, it must be important both to them and to the rest of us to treat them as far as possible as responsible agents, while making allowances for their special difficulties.

2. Determinism and Freedom[39]

Though to hold people responsible for their behaviour may make for individual and social well-being, is it open to us to do so if their behaviour is determined by their circumstances? It is sometimes said that determinism, if true, is irrelevant to the moral and legal responsibility of human agents.[40] But can this be the case, given that intelligent people have been and are concerned to show that the things that go wrong in our society are better tackled by eliminating the causes of wrongdoing than by punishing, censuring or isolating the wrongdoers?

To avoid a superficial discussion of a complex issue, I assume that it makes sense to treat people as the authors of and hence responsible for their actions. I leave open whether this is because they or their decisions cause their actions or because some non-causal relationship between them and what they do makes this a coherent view.

38. Nagel, *Mortal Questions*, above n.19, at p.36, says that "the self which acts and is the object of moral judgement is threatened with dissolution by the absorption of its acts and impulses into the class of events". This seems to me true also of the pre-moral self; the threat is to peoples' identity, not merely to how they are judged.

39. This brief discussion of a very complex topic is concerned with the hypothetical impact of determinism on our freedom – a matter of degree, since we can be more or less free – not our hypothetical freewill, which either exists or doesn't (Williams, *Humanity*, above n.8, at pp.3–8). There is no need therefore to take sides in the argument between compatibilists and incompatibilists, except to the extent that in my view determinism, if it turns out to be true, is compatible with human responsibility. The question is whether, if our decisions and actions are caused by our circumstances, this means that we are so much less free than we commonly suppose that it would be inappropriate to treat us as responsible for them.

40. P.F. Strawson "Freedom and Resentment": *Proc. Brit. Acad.* 48 (1962) 1–25 ("practically inconceivable" that it would make a difference); G. Strawson, *Freedom and Belief* (1986) ch.2; "Consciousness, Free Will and the Unimportance of Determinism", 32 *Inquiry* (1989) p.3; S.J. Morse "Diminished Capacity", in *Action and Value in Criminal Law*, above n.27, at p.239.

The worry remains that, though it may make sense to treat people as responsible for their conduct, if human actions are caused by circumstances, people are not *really* responsible for what they do. However beneficial it may be to treat them as if they were, to do so is to resort to a salutary lie. And salutary lies stop being salutary when the deception is revealed. Are people's actions in fact caused by their heredity, make-up and external circumstances? No one can be sure. Though valuable work has been done by psychologists, neurologists and sociologists the precise regularities involved, if they exist, await discovery. But it seems to make sense in each individual case to ask what reasons, conscious or unconscious, induced someone to act as they did. A person who decides to give up regular employment for freelance work can tell us the reasons that led to the decision (that they wanted more free time), or, if the reasons were partly unconscious (that they could not get their own way in the office), a colleague may be able to do so. At any rate it seems plausible to assume that some reason or reasons determined the decision to make a change. It is true that "determined" is here used in a very weak sense. When we think of a reason as explaining a decision we assume merely that it can, along with other unspecified conditions, on occasion determine a decision of that sort, not that it invariably does so, or even that it regularly does so in the absence of counteracting factors. The regularity we have in mind is far removed from the sort of regularity we suppose to exist when purely physical sequences are in question. Even so, we tend to assume that *something* determines people's decisions. That nothing determined them would imply that they were not merely unpredictable but inexplicable: a belief that would be truly alarming[41].

Should this disturb us? It seems that even "strong psychophysical explanations" bordering on psychological laws are compatible with the notions of choice, decision, action and intention to which we are committed when we treat people as responsible[42]. To suppose, as a working hypothesis, that our decisions are determined does not make it implausible or illogical to treat ourselves as the authors of our actions when we judge ourselves and others as social beings. How far

41. Hume, *Enquiries* s.VIII part i, puts this well.
42. Williams, *Humanity*, above n.8, p.8 cf. Hart, *Punishment and Responsibility. Essays in the Philosophy of Law* (1968) p.28 n.1.

back it is rational to go in tracing causes must depend on the purpose for which we want to get at the cause of something that has gone wrong. This must also apply to the causes of human conduct. It is rational to treat people as the authors of their actions in the context of a system of responsibility that we regard as valuable both for individuals and for society as a whole. To treat human action as a stopping point beyond which causal inquiries are not ordinarily pursued is sensible and indeed indispensable.[43] Perhaps we can dimly imagine an alternative world in which people were regarded as mere automata. In that world, to treat people as the authors of their actions would be a bad way of explaining events. As things are, what (if anything) determines peoples' decisions includes their make-up, preferences, and ideals, so that the hypothesis that their decisions are determined hardly makes them victims of circumstance.

All the same, worries about freedom remain. One of these concerns manipulation. Could someone who discovered the psychological laws underlying human choice, and knew enough about our make-up, manipulate us into making the choices that suited him? Perhaps, up to a point. Advertisers influence us by conscious argument and unconscious conditioning. What if those who discovered the psychological laws underlying human choice were funded by an unscrupulous advertising agency? That would be alarming, but we have ways of defending ourselves. If our decisions are determined, this only means that when we decide to do something, we regard some reason or reasons as sufficient to induce us on that occasion to reach the decision we in fact reach. It does not follow that the same reasons would be sufficient to induce another person to reach the same decision in similar circumstances or to induce us to decide the same way on another occasion. Human beings are so complex that psychological generalization from particular instances is a good deal more precarious than physical generalization. The underlying psychological laws, if they exist, must be extremely complex.

Moreover, to predict with confidence how a person is going to behave will remain difficult because people can be secretive about the details of their make-up and preferences. One aspect of the difficulty

43. Voluntary actions in particular are often treated as natural stopping-points when causal explanations are sought: Hart and Honoré, *Causation*, above n.17, at pp.41–4. But obviously there may be contexts in which it is sensible to pursue the inquiry further.

facing a knowledgeable manipulator is that any causal laws that may govern human choice are not likely to remain secret for long. Once they are made public the person who has to decide what to do has the option of falsifying any prediction based on the laws.[44] So the hypothetical laws will constantly need to be revised. In practice, then, the danger of our being manipulated to a greater extent than we are already, should rigorous psychological laws one day be discovered, must be slight.

3. Victims of Circumstance

This leaves open the question of when, if ever, it is in order to treat responsible agents in morals and in criminal law as victims of circumstance. Before imposing sanctions or attaching blame, law and morality require something more than that the person concerned is responsible for what they have done. One further requirement common to both, we have seen, is that in the circumstances the agent had the capacity to reach a rational decision about what to do. When this capacity is present, blame for bad behaviour is appropriate and criminal liability may, depending on the state of the law, be imposed. But, though capacity has often to be treated in criminal law as an all-or-nothing matter, since an offender must be found guilty or not guilty, in real life our ability to decide rationally is a matter of degree. So different degrees of blame, punishment and censure correspond to the extent to which the agent's capacity is impaired.

This implies that criminal law and morality treat agents as victims of circumstance in so far as circumstances impair their capacity to reach a rational decision. When a person suffering from impaired capacity behaves badly, this factor is taken into account in fixing the extent of criminal liability or moral censure even though it is not possible to prove that the impaired capacity was the cause of the bad behaviour. Capacity is taken into account on the retributive principle that punishment should not be disproportionate to blame. This principle acts as a constraint on the extent to which it is permissible to punish offenders in order to deter others, to promote the general welfare or to mark the community's abhorrence of what has been

44. Dennett, *Mechanism*, above n.10, at p.184 ("as an Intentional system I have an epistemic horizon that keeps my own future as an Intentional system indeterminate").

done. To apply this principle courts need to able, at least roughly, to measure desert. One way in which they do it is by making desert depend on capacity. Other things being equal, the less the defendant's capacity for rational decision the less punishment, other things being equal, the defendant deserves. Why should this be so?

To take account of capacity makes sense only if we start from a model of rational decision and behaviour. The model is that of the agent who knows or can discover the circumstances in which he or she has to reach a decision and the option or options that are available, and can think sensibly how to choose between them. This is not the way in which even the most rational person normally decides what to do. It describes rather how they can set about deciding what to do if they want to and are prepared to make the effort. It represents what is in general open to the agent rather than any process that the agent has actually gone through on the relevant occasion.

The notion of capacity involved here is that of a general capacity to do this or that, including a capacity to reason and to conform to norms. But this does not imply a capacity to have behaved differently on the occasion for which the agent is being criminally prosecuted or morally censured. The argument is one that I made as long ago as 1964;[45] Dennett has developed it further.[46] When we say that someone can do something (has the capacity to do it) we use "can" in a general, not a particular sense: we mean that the person will in general succeed in doing it if they try. To assert that someone could have acted differently on a given occasion does not mean that given the precise circumstances, including the impulses to which the agent was subject, that person could have done something different. It is rather that doing something different was not ruled out by the agent's general capacities. It is after all perfectly familiar that we fail, say, on a particular occasion to jump a six-foot ditch, though we know perfectly well that we can jump it, perhaps because we have done so before.

This general sense of "can" is the sense, I believe, in which capacity is and should be understood in criminal law. Those who are under the age of criminal responsibility or who are exempt on the ground of insanity are exempt because they do not *in general* sufficiently under-

45. "Can and Can't", *Mind* 73 (1964) pp.463–79, reprinted as Appendix, essay 7.
46. *Elbow Room*, above n.12, at pp.144–52.

stand what causes what or what options are open to them. They do not *in general* possess the balance of judgement that is needed for making sensible decisions, though they may be able to do particular things quite competently. The criminal law has of course to draw firm lines based on age or recognized mental disease, but the relation of capacity to age or mental disability is in fact a matter of degree. Criminal justice recognizes this to the extent that it is practicable to do so without endlessly prolonging investigation and trial. It commonly fixes different ages for criminal responsibility in general and for liability to certain types of punishment such as imprisonment. It draws distinctions between the mental incapacity (insanity) that excludes criminal liability altogether and lesser incapacities arising from, say, abnormality of mind that reduce the gravity of the offence. It caters for temporary mental disturbances such as underlie provocation as a defence to murder, and those milder upsets such as domestic stress that can be adduced in mitigation of punishment.

It is not easy to say why impaired capacity should lead to agents being treated as partly victims of circumstance. Why are they less at fault and less to be punished or censured than those of full capacity? To hold that they are seems to undermine responsibility as an institution that is outcome oriented: one that works by motivating success and stigmatizing failure. The link between capacity, fault and punishment or censure works against these aims, since people with impaired capacity are often more likely to offend and to do harm than those whose capacity is normal. The mentally disturbed are likely to be more dangerous to their neighbours than the mentally normal. Why, if they offend, are they to be punished or censured less than those of full capacity, who are in general less likely to do bad things? Why is it that, though such people can, with due safeguards, be rendered harmless by confinement in institutions, they cannot be blamed for what they have done, at least not to the full extent?

It seems inescapable that this is one of the ways in which regard for justice prevents us from rewarding success and penalising failure to the full extent that a goal-oriented outlook would suggest. But why exactly should law and morality, as a matter of justice, pay attention to people's capacity to control their conduct?

It is remarkably difficult to find a satisfactory answer. The best I can do is to suggest the analogy of a handicap. If life in community is to be looked on as something like a competition, in which those with impaired capacities find it more difficult to get things right, it seems fair that they should be punished or censured less when they get them wrong. They start the race from behind or have already fallen behind, so that if they stumble, any punishment should take account of the handicap that they already bear.[47] For, to the extent that they are punished, the punishment may well operate as an additional handicap, so that next time round (say when they come out of gaol) they start from still further behind. It is as if the horse carrying the heaviest weight was obliged to carry a still heavier weight. It may be that this way of looking at behaviour, in the context of fair competition, explains why, given the competitive model of society which responsibility presupposes, capacity is taken into account when punishment and censure are in issue. It is this that unites fault in the sense of getting something wrong and fault in the sense of being legally or morally to blame.

If there is this link between responsibility and capacity, certain consequences for penal policy follow that go beyond the allowance for impaired capacity that is already built into the legal system. For if account is taken of the extent to which people are handicapped by impaired capacity to control their behaviour, should the system not also take account of the extent to which they are handicapped by social and moral deprivation.[48] People can be fully rational and yet live in miserable conditions; they can belong to an underclass largely cut off from the rest of society.

To put it more precisely, people's circumstances can be such that their range of choice is limited and within that range they are subject to pressure to make wrong choices. They can have "scarcely more capacity for free choice than the person under duress".[49] Their freedom, both positive and negative, is impaired. It is not poverty as such, but this combination of restricted options and pressure to make wrong choices, that can be seen as a serious handicap in the race of

47. The idea of reformatories for young offenders rested on this notion.

48. J. Floud, "Sociology and the Theory of Responsibility: 'Social Background' " as an Excuse for Crime", in *The Science of Society and The Unity of Mankind* (ed. R. Fletcher 1974) pp.204–21 and *Psychological Medicine* 5, no.3 (1975) 227–38 sketches the idea of "social abnormality" as a conceivable defence in criminal law. I am not arguing for this, but for a candid recognition of social handicap as a mitigating factor relevant to punishment.

49. A.J. Ashworth, *Principles of Criminal Law* (2nd ed. 1995) p.245.

life. Those who suffer from it, like the incapable, are to some extent victims of circumstance.

But it is important not to succumb to the temptation of treating the restricted freedom of the socially and morally deprived as relieving them of responsibility.[50] For they, like the rest of us, benefit from the system of responsibility that gives others an incentive to treat them well and to abstain from harming them. Even more important, their self-respect and sense of identity, limited though it may be, depends on their being held responsible for their conduct. To preserve their integrity we and they must refuse to treat what they do as merely the outcome of pressure exerted by others or of the narrow range of options open to them. To hold them responsible is to respect them as people. For this reason, social and moral deprivation should be seen not as a hitherto unrecognised defence to a criminal charge, or as excusing wrongdoing, but rather as a matter to be taken into account in assessing moral guilt and in sentencing. The criminal process, against which the deprived are relatively defenceless, should acknowledge that in the race of life they start far back and that punishment, particularly imprisonment, is likely to set them further back. Probably judges do to some extent take account of social and moral deprivation, so understood. But it would be healthy to recognise this openly.

Society has to punish, because that is the only way of keeping deviance within manageable bounds. But in some ways those who are tried and convicted are like military conscripts chosen by ballot. The lot falls on them, but it could have fallen on others who committed similar offences but were not caught, or who were caught but had the intelligence and resource to conduct a sophisticated defence. Once we are alerted to the role of chance in the criminal process, it seems proper to take account of the fact that some of those prosecuted, though responsible for what they did, are handicapped by incapacity or social deprivation, and can easily be set on a downward spiral from which recovery is unlikely.

---

50. S.J. Morse, "Culpability and Control", *University of Pennsylvania Law Rev.* 142 (1994) 1587,1652–4.

7

APPENDIX

CAN AND CAN'T[1]

There is said to be a connection between the analysis of "can" and the free will problem. Whether this is so is difficult to decide, since we have not so far been very successful in trying to formulate the free will problem. The most that can be hoped, perhaps, from pulling "can" to bits is that we shall be able to see the controversy between free will and determinism more clearly, and it is with this in mind that the present exercise is undertaken.

Can (particular) and can (general). It is convenient to begin by making a distinction between two uses of "can" that I label "particular" and "general". Later it will emerge that these two uses are interconnected. Indeed, no clear account of the one can be given without an explanation of the other.

I begin with "can" (particular), which is so labelled because it is used primarily in connection with particular actions. Though not necessarily the commonest use of "can", there is a sense in which it is the most fundamental, and for this reason it is treated first. "Can" (particular) may be illustrated from an example suggested by Austin,[2] who unfortunately fails to draw the proper conclusions from it. Suppose a competent golfer must hole a short putt in order to win a game. No doubt there is a sense in which a competent golfer can hole a short putt: he has the ability to do so, and there is nothing to prevent him exercising his ability on this occasion. But in another sense, with which we are now concerned, his competence as a golfer does not conclude the matter. In this sense, namely the *particular* sense of "can", it is proper to ask of even a competent golfer addressing himself to a short putt "can he sink the putt?" and it is proper for him to

1. First published in *Mind* 73 (1964) 463–479.
2. J. Austin, *Philosophical Papers* (1961) p.166, n.1.

assert "I can sink it", or "I ought to be able to sink it", or "I think I can sink it".

In this sense "can" is almost equivalent to "will" and has a predictive force. Indeed in French the future "Est-ce qu'il pourra?" would be correct. This presents a difficulty for anyone who thinks of the "can" notion as closely tied to some general and unvarying capacity of the agent. On the contrary: "can he sink this putt?" when "can" is particular, is like, "will he sink this putt?", the tacit assumption being that he will try to sink it, which we can take for granted in the context. Conversely, "he can't sink it" virtually means "he won't sink it", again on the assumption that he will try.

The use of "can" (particular) is not confined to cases where the action in question has not yet been attempted. Suppose that someone has succeeded in doing something. It is perfectly correct to use "could" or "was able to" to express this. Thus "I could see you in the undergrowth" is properly said only when I have succeeded in seeing you. When ordinary verbs of action are used, English requires not "could" but "was able to" in such contexts, as in "I was able to overtake him". In French the ordinary word for "can" is correct, as in "J'ai pu le rattraper". "J'ai su" is also correctly used to express "can" (particular) when the action has already been done, as in "J'ai su me cacher". In all these cases it is implied that I have succeeded in doing the thing in question; we cannot say, in this sense of "was able", "I was able to do so-and-so, but did not in fact do it".

To illustrate the use of "could not" (particular) I return to the example of the short putt. If the golfer tried his best to sink the putt and failed, then, in the particular sense of "can", he could not sink it. He would be entitled to explain that, try as he might, he could not manage to succeed. "I could not make it". Such statements can only correctly be made if the agent has been unsuccessful despite the fact that he has tried.

To summarize the use of "can" (particular) in relation to particular actions: success or failure, on the assumption that an effort has been or will be made, is the factor that governs the use of the notion. If the agent tried and failed, he could not do the action: if he tried and succeeded, he was able to do it. If he will fail however hard he tries, he cannot do it; if he will succeed provided he tries, he can.

It is time to turn to "can" (general), which is so labelled because it is most commonly used in connection with types of action rather than particular actions. "Can" in this sense is used to assert a general competence, ability or skill in the performance of some type of action. If a person is a competent golfer, "he can hole a short putt" must be true; otherwise he would not be competent. What we usually mean by saying that a person can do an action of a certain type is not that he may do it, that it is on the cards that will do such an action, but rather that he normally succeeds in doing it when he tries.[3] If a typist claims that she can type sixty words a minute, she is asserting that normally or on average she types at that rate, when she wants to, not merely that she has once managed by a fluke to get in sixty words to the minute.

It is true that "can" statements, where "can" is general, are sometimes qualified by adverbs such as "invariably", "occasionally", or the like. We may say "he can occasionally sink a six-foot putt" or "he can invariably sink a six-foot putt". But if no such qualification is added, it is implied that the "can" statement refers to the agent's normal or standard performance when he tries. This is true at least in the cases where "can" is unemphatic. If, on the other hand, emphasis is placed on "can", as in "he *can* make a good after dinner speech", the implication is that he does not usually make a good speech, either because he does not try, or because on the few occasions on which he speaks well, this is attributable to luck, that is, to some rare circumstance or combination of circumstances.

Whereas a condition sufficient for asserting "he can (general) do such-and-such a type of action" is that, when the agent tries, he normally succeeds in doing an action of that type, the conditions for asserting "he can't do such-and-such a type of action" are that, when the agent tries to do an action of that type, he always or nearly always fails. It is perhaps not necessary that the agent should never succeed. "Can you go round this course in under ninety?" "No, I can't, though I once did it in 88". When evidence of actual performance is not available, it is a sufficient ground for asserting "he can (general) do such-and-such a type of action" that, if he tried to, he normally would succeed, and a sufficient ground for asserting "he can't do such-and-such a type of action" that, if he tried, he would always or nearly always fail.

Statements involving "can" (general) may be put in the future or past as well as the present: "I could run a hundred yards in eleven

3. All the better if he succeeds in doing it, when he wants to, without trying.

seconds when I was younger", "I shall be able to play the harp in twelve months time".

Though "can" (general) is primarily used of types of action, it has a secondary application to particular actions. Thus, if a golfer "can" (general) hole six-foot putts, he "can" (general) hole this six-foot putt, provided there is nothing in the special circumstances of the case to prevent him doing so on this occasion. Conversely a golfer who "can't" (general) hole six-foot putts "can't" (general) hole this six-foot putt unless there is something in the special circumstances to enable him to do so.

"Can" (general), when used of particular actions, differs from "can" (particular), when used of particular actions, in that its correct use does not depend on actual or prospective success or failure. "He can hole this six-foot putt" may be true, in the general sense of "can" because he usually does hole a putt of that sort and there is nothing abnormal to prevent him doing so this time, although the golfer, if he tried, would in practice fail to sink it. It is true that, if we *know* that the golfer will fail to sink the putt, we must not say "he can hole it". We must not use the word "can", since "can" is used in English in such a way in relation to particular actions that "can" is inconsistent with failure, "can't" with success. But we may nevertheless express the *notion* of "can" (general) by saying "he has the ability to hole it" or "he has the capacity to hole it" and such statements will carry with them the ordinary implications of "can" statements in the sphere of responsibility. Thus, if the golfer had the capacity to hole the putt but could not (particular) hole it, though he tried, he may nevertheless be held responsible or blamed for his failure, because he could have holed it, though he is not to blame to the same extent as in the case where he did not even try.

"Can" (general) is used not only of future actions but of particular past actions. Here two different cases need to be separated. First, if the agent did not attempt the action, we may say "he could have done it", in one sense of that expression,[4] viz. "he was in a position to do it", or "there was nothing to prevent him doing it". This may properly be said if the action is of the sort that the agent manages to do in

4. "He could have done it" may also mean (i) "he would have been in a position to do it", which is compatible with "he would not in fact have succeeded in doing it" or (ii) "he would have been able to do it", which is incompatible with "he would not have succeeded in doing it, if, in the hypothetical circumstances, he had tried".

normal circumstances when he tries and if there was nothing unusual to stop him on the occasion in question. Contrast with this use of "can" (general) in relation to past actions the use of "can" (particular) in expressions such as "he was able to do so-and-so", which is compatible only with the agent's having succeeded.

Secondly, if the agent attempted the action, either he succeeded, in which case "can" (particular) is used, or he failed, in which case we must say "he could have done it, if . . .". "If" here introduced an explanation of the agent's failure. For example, when our friend the competent golfer fails to hole a short putt, we may say "he could have holed it if he had kept his feet together" or "if he had not become rattled". One point about this form of expression is that "he could have, if . . ." does not entail "he would have, if" . . . even on the assumption that he tried. The "can" is general, not particular. Contrast "he would have been able to, if . . ." which cannot properly be asserted, unless it is the case that the agent would have done the thing in question if the condition had been fulfilled and he had tried. "He could have, if he had kept his feet together", is true if it is the case that he had the necessary ability and that, if he had kept his feet together, there would have been nothing to prevent him, which does not entail that the golfer would actually have sunk the putt, even if he had kept his feet together.

There is something at first sight paradoxical about the use of "can" (general) in relation to particular actions that the agent has attempted and failed to achieve. If the agent did not attempt the action but there was nothing to prevent him doing so, we may categorically assert "he could have done it"; but if he tried and failed we say "he could have done it, if . . .". Yet the conditions for asserting general "can" of a particular action are (1) that the action is of the sort that the agent normally achieves when he tries, and (2) that there is nothing in the circumstances to prevent the agent's succeeding on this occasion. How can these conditions vary according to whether the agent has attempted the action? The solution is that factors which in prospect are not thought of as preventing success, since it is not certain that they will be present, are in retrospect seen to have done so. We say of an agent that he "can" (general) do a particular action because we do not know that he will make a mistake or become rattled. In the event we discover that there was a factor present which prevented success and so we must modify our general "can" statement.

The foregoing discussion has been intended to bring out a persistent ambiguity in the notion of "can". This is quite clearly revealed if we examine "can" statements about particular actions that the agent has tried but failed to do. In such cases it is often the case that the agent could not (particular) do the action, because he tried and failed, but that he could have done it (general), if he had not made a mistake, because he was in a position to do it in the sense that, given his normal level of achievement, there was nothing to prevent him doing so. In English the connection between "can" and achievement is so strong that we cannot describe the situation by saying "he could and he could not". We must rather have recourse to "he was in a position to, but did not mange to . . ." or "he could have, but did not manage to". In Latin, according to Austin, *potuit sed non potuit* would apparently be in order.

Again, if we think of a particular action not yet attempted it may be true that the agent, unknown to us at the time, "can't" (particular) do it, since if he tries he will fail, but at the same time "can" (general) do it, because he has the ability or skill and there is nothing certainly to prevent him. If, however, we knew that he would fail, we should have to withdraw the "can" (general) statement, and substitute something like "he has the ability to do this" or "he could do it if he performed as he normally does". This demonstrates, once more, the strong connection between "can" in English and actual performance.

This strong connection must not be allowed to obscure the fact that the notion of "can" possesses a systematic ambiguity and that this gives it its force as a instrument for assessing conduct. When "can" (general) is used of a particular action the agent is judged by his normal performance, whilst when "can" (particular) is used he is judged by his performance on this occasion, on the assumption in both cases that he tries. The fact that an agent can't (particular) or could not (particular) do the action does not exculpate him entirely if he could (general) have done it; it merely mitigates the blame. Not trying is worse that losing one's head or adopting a faulty method, but it is not the only ground for blame.

If. It is clear that the ground or conditions for asserting "can" statements, both particular and general, often involve "ifs". What sort of "ifs" are involved? Are they always involved or only sometimes?

To take "can" (particular) first, the grounds for asserting "he can do this particular action" may be that, if he tries, he will do it, or that, if he tried, he would do it. But when "can" (particular) is used of past actions, the ground for asserting it does not involve "if". Thus, neither "he was able to do it" nor "he could not do it" requires for its truth the truth of any proposition involving "if".

Again, the grounds for asserting that an agent "can" (general) do a type of action may be that, when he tries, he normally succeeds in doing it or that, if he tried, he normally would succeed. So in both cases, the grounds for asserting the "can" statement may involve the truth of a hypothetical statement or may not, according to the context and circumstances. But no conclusion can be drawn from this about the character of the "can" statements themselves. For instance, it would be strange if the assertion "he can sink six-foot putts" were treated as having a different character according as the evidence on which it was based was that the golfer habitually sank six-foot putts when he tried to or that, though he never tried to sink a six-foot putt, he habitually sank ten-foot putts, from which one could deduce that, if he tried to sink six-foot putts, he would normally succeed. Indeed, the classification of statements into categorical and hypothetical does not usefully apply to statements of capacity and disposition and there seems no good reason for forcing "can" statements into these moulds.

When the grounds for asserting "can" statements involve "ifs", and the fulfilment of the hypothesis can be taken for granted, the assertion that an agent "can" (particular) do something has almost the force of an assertion that he is doing or will do it. This can be illustrated from examples that involve not ordinary actions but sensation or knowledge. Thus, "I can tell you something fascinating about her" is almost equivalent to "I will tell you something fascinating about her" and "I can imagine how embarrassed you must feel about the whiskey" is almost equivalent to "I imagine how embarrassed you feel", since it can be taken for granted that I want to impart the information in the first case and to feel sympathetic in the second. In such instances the statement involving "can" (particular) are almost equivalent to a direct assertion. Conversely, when the nonfulfilment of the condition can be taken for granted, the "can" statement may have the force of a negation, as in "I could ruin you if I were that sort of person", which expands into "I can (particular) ruin you, as you would realise if I were that sort of person, but, as I am not, I shall not ruin you".

So far the "ifs" we have encountered have been of the familiar variety. Austin thought that a special sort of "if" was involved in some "can" statements.[5] There is, indeed, a class of statements, of which "I can if I choose", "I can if I like", "he can if he wants" and "he could if he tried" provide examples that look rather puzzling. Very often the conditions for asserting "can" (particular) involve the truth of a statement of the form "if the agent tried he would" and the conditions for asserting "can" (general) often involve the truth of a statement that, if the agent tried, he normally would succeed in doing the type of action in question. In such cases the phrases "if he tried etc." look superfluous, because trying is already implied in the assertion "he could". So what is added to "he could" by "if he tried?" Again, if a person tries to do something, he chooses to do it, and so a similar objection can be raised to "I can if I choose". The same is not quite true of "want" and "like" since we may choose to try to do what we do not want or like to do, but, even so, wanting and liking normally accompany choosing and trying.

The apparent puzzle arises from the fact that statements of the sort being considered are elliptical. The "if" clauses refer to the proof, not the truth of the "can" statements. Thus "I can if I choose" may be expended to read "I can, and if I choose to do the action, you will see that I can, because I shall succeed". "He could if he tried" expands to "he can, and if he tried to do the action he would realise that he can, because he would succeed". It is the elliptical form of the expression, not any peculiarity of "if", that accounts for the surface oddness of such statements. There are many analogous forms of expression in English, not all of which involve "can". Austin mentions[6] "I paid you back yesterday, if you remember", which expands into "I paid you back yesterday, as you will readily admit, if you remember the incident". Another example is "I want to take a holiday if I can".

The investigation of these odd-looking sentences involving "can" really supports the analysis of "can" sentences in terms of effort and success or failure, since they would have no real force unless it were the case that, on the assumption that the agent tries, success or failure determines the truth of the "can" (particular) statement.

---

5. *Philosphical Papers*, p.160.
6. *Philosophical Papers*, p.161, n.1.

Try. The grounds for asserting "can" (particular) and "can" (general) both sometimes involve the notion of trying. A person "can" (particular) do a particular action if, *inter alia*, it is the case that he would do it if he tried. A person "can" (general) do a certain type of action if, *inter alia*, it is the case that when he tries he normally succeeds in doing actions of that type and "can" (general) do a particular action of that type if it is also true that there is nothing special in the circumstances to prevent him succeeding on this occasion.

In analysing "can" we are therefore involved in analysing "try". It is true that the grounds for asserting "can" statements do not always involve "try", and this for two reasons. Sometimes, as in statements about past actions, such as "I was able to overtake him", the element of trying has been merged in the successful achievement. In other cases the action is not like an ordinary action and the notion of trying does not apply to it. This is true of sense perception in particular. Expression such as "can see" are sometimes used in a way in which, by implication, trying is part of the ground for the assertion, sometimes not. We may contrast, for instance, "I cannot see my spectacles anywhere", which implies that I have been trying to find them, looking for them, with "I can see a No. 2 bus coming", which does not necessarily imply that I have tried to find, or looked for one. It is correct, at least in English, to say "I can see a No. 2 bus" if in fact I see one, just as it is correct to say "I can (general) hear the train whistle on a still day", if it is the case that, in appropriate conditions, I do hear it, even without listening for it or straining my ears. To use "can" is rather pointless[7] unless there is something difficult or unusual about what the agent does, and this accounts, no doubt, for the fact that, for instance, the French for "I can see a No. 2 bus coming" would normally be "Je vois un autobus . . ." and not "Je peux voir. . . ."

This does not invalidate the analysis of "can" statements suggested earlier. It merely shows that, while for ordinary actions we are justified in asserting "he can" (particular) if it is the case that, if he tries, he will succeed, in the case of sense perception we will often be justified in asserting "he can" merely on the ground that, in suitable conditions, he will do the thing in question. *Mutatis mutandis*, the same will hold good of statements involving "can" (general). This

7. Perhaps not utterly. "Can" may have the function of emphasising success not merely when the task if difficult in itself but when the conditions for success are seldom present. The bus may be a long time coming.

reinforces the notion that there is a close link between "can" statements and success or failure.

We may now turn to the notion of trying. A rather curious question confronts us at the outset. Is it necessary, in order that a person can do something, that he should be able to try to do it? May "can he do this?" coexist with "He cannot try to do it?" At first sight we are plainly inclined to answer "no". An example will help. Suppose that the way to sink the crucial putt is for the golfer to apply a given momentum X to the golf ball. If the golfer cannot impart just that momentum, it seems obvious that he cannot (particular) sink the putt.

Of course it does not follow that the golfer could not (general) have sunk it. If, then, we provisionally say that trying to sink the putt amounts, in this case, to imparting momentum X to the ball, the fact that the golfer can (particular) strike the ball with momentum X is a necessary condition of his being able (particular) to hole the putt but not of his having the capacity (general) to hole it.

It seems that the analysis of "can he try" will be relevant to statements involving "can" (particular). Suppose we adopt for "can he try to do a particular action?" an analysis similar to that adopted for "can he do a particular action?" Then "he can try to do so-and-so", when "can" is particular, will be true if and only if it is the case that, if he tried to try to do so-and-so, he would try to do so-and-so. Has such a hypothesis any sensible meaning? Are we led into a vicious regress of ascending powers of "try"?

We are and we are not. It seems reasonable, in the analysis of "try", to make use of the legal analysis of attempts, since the differences between trying and attempting to do something may safely be disregarded for present purposes. According to this analysis, to try to do a particular action involves (a) intending to do it and (b) taking a step towards the achievement of it, by doing something that will lead or that the agent believes will lead directly or indirectly to the action being accomplished. How "proximate" the step need be to the final aim is legally important but does not concern us here.

If the agent makes a mistake about the means to be adopted for achieving his aim, he can't (particular) do the particular action, because if he tries, he will fail. In such cases there is no need to inquire whether the agent can try, since, even if he can, he will not manage to perform the action. I confine myself, therefore, to cases where the agent has hit on a suitable way of trying to perform the action. I use the letter "Y" to designate a suitable means for performing a particular action. We can then split the question "Can the agent try to perform the particular action?" into two parts (1) can he intend to perform the action and (2) can he do Y? Only if both parts are answered in the affirmative may we conclude that the agent can try to perform the completed action.

The second part is best tackled first. There is no doubt that it involves us in a regress. Trying to shoot someone involves firing at him. Trying to fire involves pressing the trigger. Trying to press the trigger involves grasping the revolver . . . . If we continue to pursue the sequence we land in a paradox, for in one sense there is no staring point, while in another there is.

Suppose we take provisionally, as a starting point in the shooting example, the action of rising from one's chair to go to the shop to buy the revolver to shoot the victim. In one sense the action of trying to rise from one's chair just consists in telling oneself to get up, in sending a message to that effect and hoping that one has not become paralysed. I use the letter "I" to designate an action of this sort, one that is intended to initiate an ordinary action and which consists in directing messages or orders to oneself. The question to be answered is: can an agent try to do an "I" action? Can I send myself a message to tell myself to get up? The question seems senseless, since there is no difference, in this context, between sending myself a message or order to get up and sending myself a message to send myself a message to that effect. Trying to do an "I" action is the same thing as doing an "I" action, and where an "I" action is the means to performing the particular action in which we are interested, there is no difference between trying to perform the action and trying to try to perform it. It follows that it is impossible to analyse "can he do an "I" action?" in terms of trying. It is rather that, if the agent is prevented from doing such an action, he cannot do it, while if he is not prevented from doing it, he can do it.

I will return to "prevention" later, but let us first look at an alternative interpretation of notions such as trying to rise from one's chair. There may well be a recipe or technique for getting oneself to do such an action. For instance, to rise from a chair one may try shaking oneself, removing an obstacle, drinking a cup of coffee. On this interpretation of "trying to rise", it is not an "I" action, but is like any other intermediate "Y" action which is a means towards or stage in the accomplishment of the action in question, here "shooting the victim". There must be few if any actions for the doing of which no recipe or technique can be suggested, so that in general a proposed action of the "I" type may be interpreted as an action of the intermediate "Y" type. If this is done, the question "can the agent do so-and-so?" may lead to an infinite regress, since it is possible that an indefinite number of questions about intermediate "Y" actions, each of which is conceived as a means to the accomplishment of the previously mentioned action, may be answered in the affirmative.

Questions such as "can the agent try to rise from the chair in which he is sitting?" may therefore sometimes have to be answered in two different ways, according to the interpretation adopted. If the agent is prevented from trying directly, by an "I" type action, to rise, for instance through extreme fatigue or a psychological block, he cannot try to rise and so can't (particular) rise and can't shoot the victim. But it may be that, though he cannot now try to rise, he could now be trying to if he had gone about it the right way previously, by adopting the appropriate technique. If, in addition, he normally can (general) rise from a chair, then we are justified in asserting that he could now be rising, if he had taken the proper steps, though as things are he cannot rise. Just as we contrast particular "can" statements, for which present achievement sets the standard, with general "can" statements, for which normal achievement sets the standard, so we may contrast immediate "can" statements, such as "he can't now try to rise" with projected "can" statements, such as "he could now be trying to rise, if in the past . . .", in which capacity is related to a longer period of time, and so projected in time. It is easy to see that these projected "can" statements, like the similar statements considered earlier, of the form "he could have done so-and-so, if" are applications of can (general) to particular actions in cases where the agent, in the particular sense of "can", can't or could not do the thing in question.

To recapitulate, the statement that an agent can (particular) do so-and-so seems to require at least the truth of the statement that the agent can try to do so-and-so. What sort of "can" is involved in "can try"? If "can" is particular, we may, as we press the inquiry back, come fairly quickly to an initiating action such as the agent could not do, because he was prevented from doing it. Alternatively, if the initiating action is interpreted instead as an intermediate "Y" action, we may pursue the inquiry farther into the past. Very often, however, we shall ultimately be faced with a question involving "prevent" and it is to the analysis of this that I now turn.

When is a person prevented from doing an initiating "I" action? It will not help to have recourse to the notion of trying, because trying to do an "I" action is indistinguishable from doing it. We are obliged to say, rather, that a person is not prevented from doing an "I" action if it is the case that, if he wanted to, he would do it, since he is not paralysed, and that he can want to do it. Conversely, a person is prevented from doing an "I" action if it is the case that, even if he wanted to, he would not do it.

This drives us back on the analysis of "can the agent want to do the action?" At first sight it seems senseless to suggest that a person can want what he does not want, or can fail to want what he does want. Either I want to learn Russian or I do not. Either I want to take heroin or I do not. But while it is true that a person does not change his wants by wanting, trying or hoping to want something different, it would be false to maintain that there are no techniques available to us for changing our wants. I may know that, though I do not now want to learn Russian, I could get myself to want it by reading more Russian literature in translation, and I may know that though I now want to take heroin, I could get myself to stop wanting it by taking a cure. Reading the Russian novels or taking the cure would be ways of trying to change my wants. Hence I can often, indirectly, get myself to want something that I do not now want, and I could often, by taking action in the past, have got myself now to be wanting something that I do not in fact now want.

The upshot of the discussion seems to be that we may often have to return an equivocal answer to questions of the form "can he want to do an 'I' action?" and so to the question whether the agent can try to do so-and-so, and ultimately to the question the agent can (particular) do so-and-so. For if the "can" in "can want" is taken in the particular and immediate sense, we may have to admit that the agent could not want what he did not want and cannot want what he does not want, while if we take "can" in the general and projected sense, we may have to maintain that the agent could have wanted or could now be wanting what he did not or does not want, if he had taken appropriate steps in the past. The same question may of course be put of the steps that the agent could have taken in the past, and so the answer "he could" in relation to any particular step will never be conclusive of the whole inquiry, whereas the answer "he could not" will be[8] conclusive of the "can" question, though not necessarily of the question of responsibility. Hence we arrive at the perhaps surprising conclusion that questions of the type "can the agent do so-and-so?" where "can" is particular, cannot be conclusively answered unless the answer is "no".

This is surprising, because in real life we often give the answer "yes" to such questions. The answer "yes" must therefore rest on the assumption that, however often we repeat the projection, the answer "yes" will continue to be given in reply to the question "could the agent have taken the steps that would have enabled him to accomplish the intermediate action?" This assumption dispenses us from carrying the inquiry beyond the immediate background. In ordinary life we answer "yes" to the question "can the agent do so-and-so?" when it is clear that, if he tried to do so-and-so, he would succeed, if it is also the case that there is no immediate or obvious reason why the agent can't try to do so-and-so. A full justification for the answer would, theoretically, involve the proposition that, however far we pressed the inquiry whether the agent could try, affirmative answers would be forthcoming, always on the assumption that projection was allowed. It seems therefore, that when an affirmative statement involving "can" (particular) is made, an infinite regress is always involved. This regress may be translated, in terms of responsibility, into the rough presumption that "you can always try".

A further conclusion may be drawn from the foregoing analysis. When the conditions that justify an affirmative answer to a particular "can" statement are listed, they will be found notionally to include the fact that an indefinite number of projected "can" statements have been answered in the affirmative. These projected "can" statements are applications of "can" (general). We may deduce that, just as the analysis of "can" (general) involves "can" (particular), so the analysis of "can" (particular) involves "can" (general). The two uses of "can", though distinguishable, are interdependent. In fact "can" combines in

8. Because "he could not" will be true if *either* he could not try *or* he could try but without success, whereas "he could" is true only if he could try.

a subtle way assessments of conduct in which achievement on the particular occasion is decisive with those in which the agent's normal achievements set the standard. Since we presume that people have the same general capacities until the contrary is shown, we may fairly say that the tendency of the "can" concept is to apply pressure towards uniform standards of conduct.

Intend. One element in trying, so far left on one side, is that the agent must intend to succeed. "Can he try to do so-and-so?" leads us to "Can he intend to do so-and-so?", which sounds an odd question. One reason for the oddness is much the same as in the case of "want". We intend to do what we intend to do, and do not intend to so what we do not intend to do; we do not change our intentions by wanting, liking or hoping to intend something different. On the other hand, we can often get ourselves to change our intentions, to change our minds, by a suitable technique. At present I do not intend to go to London tomorrow and it is no use sending myself messages urging myself to intend it. On the other hand, I can think of ways in which I might get myself to intend to go to London tomorrow, such as thinking of a place where I can eat a Chateaubriand steak. Hence I may be justified in saying "I could now be intending to go to London" or more naturally "I might have decided to go to London, if I had previously thought of the juicy steak". Though in the immediate and particular sense of "can" I can't intend what I do not intend, it may often be true that in a projected and general sense I could.

Often we acquire intentions, so to speak, unreflectively, without any conscious process of deliberation, choosing or making up our minds. In these straightforward cases there is no need to add to the foregoing analysis. A little must be said, however, of cases in which an intention is acquired by a process of deliberation or choice. In such cases, the question "can the agent intend to do so-and-so?" leads to the question "can he choose?" or "can he decide?" Such questions may be interpreted as meaning "can he reach a decision?" or "can he make up his mind?" Now reaching a decision or making up one's mind is not in principle different from other actions. One can certainly try to reach a decision and there are techniques for doing so. Trying might consist, for instance, in drawing up a list of pros and cons, discussing the matter with a friend or thinking it over carefully.

On another interpretation, which is of more concern to us here, "can he decide?" means "can he decide in favour of course A rather than course B?" or "can he choose A in preference to B?" Such questions may be interpreted in a projected sense, since we know of techniques for altering our preferences. Suppose, however, that we take them in an immediate particular sense. What are the criteria for saying that an agent can here and now choose A rather than B, and at the same time B rather than A, so that he has a genuine choice? Surely the criterion must be that nothing prevents him from choosing either. He is not overcome by extreme fatigue or a psychological block. The analysis of "prevent" in this context will be the same as was put forward earlier. An agent is prevented from choosing a course of action if it is the case that even if he wanted to, he would not choose it, and is not prevented from choosing it, if it is the case that if he wanted to, he would choose it. For the agent not to be prevented, it is also necessary that he should be able to want to choose the course of action in question. "Being able to want to do something" is, again, susceptible of a double interpretation. For a person to have a genuine choice between alternatives, so that he is not prevented from choosing either, we must assume that, if the question "can he want?" is treated as projected, however far we pursue it the answer "yes" will be returned. In terms of responsibility we might express this assumption in the form of the rough presumption that "we could always have arranged our wants differently". In order to return the answer "yes", to the question "can the agent choose A rather than B also B rather than A, so that he has a genuine choice?", we must notionally be satisfied than an indefinite series of projected "can" questions would be answered in the affirmative. In practice, we dispense with this and are satisfied if there is no immediate or obvious obstacle to a given choice.

Conclusions

If the foregoing analysis is correct some conclusions may perhaps be drawn.

1. The answer to "can" questions is often taken as the basis for assessing a person's responsibility for his conduct. Is this a sensible procedure? One relevant consideration is presumably the extent to which statements involving "can" (particular) are genuinely factual. A distinction must here be drawn between negative "can" statements that are sometimes genuinely factual, and positive "can" statements that

rest on unverifiable assumptions and which, it seems to me, we cannot strictly speaking know to be true or false. Another relevant consideration is the ambiguity of "can" questions. There is often, in discussions of responsibility, an oscillation between "can" (particular) and "can" (general). So far as "can" (general) is used to settle responsibility, it is tacitly assumed that a person's conduct may properly be judged according to his normal standard of achievement and so indirectly by the standard of the average man. This assumption must be justified by something other than the ordinary use of "can".

2. Nothing in the use of "can" rules out determinism, if determinism is formulated in the following way: when we think and say we have a choice or are free to decide, it is always the case that we are prevented from choosing or deciding on any course of action except one; and the course to be chosen is as predictable as any other event given sufficient information.

This needs a little elaboration. I am offered beer or whiskey. I choose beer. Could I have chosen whiskey? According to ordinary usage, I could have chosen whiskey if I was not prevented, according to the criteria already discussed, from choosing it. Suppose, however, that it can be shown that before I "choose" beer, my brain exhibits electrical disturbances characteristic of "about to ask for beer" and inconsistent with "about to ask for whiskey". Suppose, further, that this is shown to be an instance of a general truth about what we call choice and decision, and suppose that "choices" and "decisions" turn out to be capable of being predicted independently of the agent's own account of the process.

We should then come to reinterpret the experiences we now call "making up our minds"; and "reaching a decision". We should come to think of them as more like "becoming conscious of our intention". To accommodate the change, we should need to reinterpret our notion of intention: but, as we already talk about unconscious intentions and motives, this need not disturb us very much. We should come to think of ourselves as prevented from "choosing" or "deciding" in any way except one: but although this was in principle determinable in advance, we should often not know how to determine it, because we should not be conscious of the factors that prevented us from "choosing" otherwise. There would still be a distinction between those cases in which we were conscious of the preventing factors and those in which we were unconscious of them; but no doubt the notion of "preventing" would have to be readjusted to meet the new situation.

In such a world "can" would continue to represent a technique, not necessarily less successful than at present, for securing the observance of uniform standards of conduct. Many of our present concepts would have to be stretched or compressed. But there is no reason to assume that our present scheme of concepts is adequate.

INDEX